# How Do We Tell the Children?

# How Do We Tell the Children?

*A Step-by-Step Guide for*
*Helping Children Two to Teen*
*Cope When Someone Dies*

THIRD EDITION

## Dan Schaefer, Ph.D.
## and
## Christine Lyons

NEWMARKET PRESS • NEW YORK

THIRD EDITION

Copyright ©1986, 1988, 1993, 2001 by Dan Schaefer

This book is published simultaneously in
the United States and in Canada.

10 9 8 7 6 5 4 3 2 1 paperback
10 9 8 7 6 5 4 3 2 1 hardcover

Library of Congress Cataloging-in-Publication Data

Schaefer, Dan.
    How do we tell the children?
    Bibliography: p.
    Includes index.
    1. Children and death.  2.Death—Psychological ✓
aspects.  3.Bereavement—Psychological aspects.  4. Parent
and child.  I. Lyons, Christine  II. Title.
BF723.D3S33 1986        155.9'37.        85-61816
ISBN 1-55704-425-2 (pb)        ISBN 1-55704-430-9 (hc)

QUANTITY PURCHASES

Companies, professional groups, clubs, and other organizations may qualify for special terms when ordering quantities of this title. For information, write the Special Sales Department, Newmarket Press, 18 East 48th Street, New York, NY 10017, call (212) 832-3575, fax (212) 832-3629, or e-mail mailbox@newmarketpress.com.

www.newmarketpress.com

Manufactured in the United States

To contact the author, please call (212) 265-1888,
e-mail danconco@msn.com, or write to:
Dan Schaefer, Ph.D., Peak Performance Strategies,
161 West 61st Street, New York, NY 10023.

TO OUR CHILDREN:

*Andrea, Daniel, Pamela, Mark, David, and Shawn Schaefer*
*and Sean, Bridget, and Brendan Lyons*

---

## *Acknowledgments for the Third Edition*

Special thanks to Dr. Lisa Hudson, Ph.D., Hudson Associates, Augusta, Georgia:

A friend and colleague whose contribution to this work is a monument to her dedication to her own healing, to her son, to her private and corporate clients who have learned to nurture themselves, and to those suffering loss and life transition.

Level 1 Trauma Center, Lutheran Medical Center, Brooklyn, New York: Anthony Acinapura, M.D., Chairman, Department of Surgery; Ramanathan Raju, M.D., FRCS, FACS, FICS, Director of Trauma; Charusheela Andaz, M.D.; Fred Nenner, CSW, Director of Clinical Resource Management Center, who illustrated the heart of a trauma team; Giuseppe Constantino, Ph.D., Director of Mental Health; and the Pastoral Care Department, which has been a valuable resource throughout all three editions of this work.

Pat Travis Rosenberg, Sea Cliff, N.Y., for sharing her poem, "Life Goes On," from her book *Flying Through Clouds*, written in memory of her son David.

Keith Hollaman, Editor; Esther Margolis, Publisher, Newmarket Press.

Kimberly Fraioli ATR-BC, LPC, Director of Expressive Therapies, Northeast Center for Trauma Recovery, Greenwich, Connecticut; Orly Knigin MSW, New York, New York; Sharami Kerr MSC, Director of Heartbridge Center, New York, New York; John Weshons, Open Heart Interventions, Little Falls, New Jersey; Lu Redmond, R.N., M.S., LMFT, Clearwater, Florida; Mark Lerner, Ph.D., Brad Lindell, Ph.D. and Joseph Volpe, Ph.D., American Academy of Experts in Traumatic Stress, Commack, New York; Barrie Sue Zicherman, Z Associates, Performance Enhancement in Education, Roslyn, New York; David Endler, Ph.D.; Helen Fitzgerald, CDE, Training Director, American Hospice Foundation; Gabriel Moran, New York University School of Education; Marv and Joy Johnson, The Centering Bereavement Resource Center, Omaha, Nebraska.

## *Acknowledgments for the Second Edition*

I would like to thank the following experts who gave me guidance and advice in the preparation of this updated edition: Carol Becker and Josephine DiVernieri, Brooklyn Cancer Institute; Constance Butherus, R.N., M.A., Hunterdon Developmental Center, Clinton, New Jersey; Carol Cohen, R.N., and Mark Evans, M.S.W., C.S.W., Lutheran Medical Center, Brooklyn, New York; Barbara Dane, D.S.W., Associate Professor, New York University School of Social Work; Richard Ellis, Ph.D., New York University; David Endler, Ph.D.; Beth Evans, bereavement consultant, Spring Valley, New York; Roberta Halporn, M.A., Director of the Center for Thanatology Research and Education; Jeffrey Kauffman, M.A., Center for the Care of Community Institutions, St. Peters, Pennsylvania; Stephen Kuwent, Certified School Psychologist, State of New Jersey; Erica Leeuwenburgh, M.P.S., and Judy Solomon, M.S.W., Tomorrow's Children Institute, Hackensack Medical Center, Hackensack, New Jersey; Michael Lipson, Ph.D., Senior Psychologist, Department of Pediatrics, Harlem Hospital, New York City; Eileen McGrath, Ph.D.; Barbara Meyers, Director of the Holistic Animal Consulting Center, Staten Island, New York; Ken Moses, Ph.D., Resource Network, Evanston, Illinois; Ruth Rothbart-Mayer, M.S.W., C.S.W., co-founder of Mayer-Avedon Women's Support Group; Roberta Schaefer, M.S.W., C.S.W., Baldwin Harbor, New York; Donna Schuurman, Executive Director of the Dougy Center, Portland, Oregon; Robert Stevenson, Ph.D.; the Reverend Jack Stouffer and the Reverend Maury Drumm, Department of Pastoral Care, Lutheran Medical Center, Brooklyn, New York; Margaret Zamierowski, M.P. S., the Brooklyn Hospice, Brooklyn, New York; and a special thanks to my editor, Keith Hollaman.

## Acknowledgments for the First Edition

In the course of developing my program and this book, I received guidance and assistance from a great many people. I would like to thank the following: Alan J. Barnett, Ph.D., National Psychological Association for Psychoanalysis; John Brogan and Ula Maiden, Strang Middle School, Yorktown Heights, New York; Rudolph Calabrese, Ph.D.; Bruce Danto, M.D.; the Reverend Ingimar DeRidder, Brooklyn Baptist Church; the Reverend Edward Dougherty, Immaculate Conception Seminary, Huntington, New York; Hal Fishkin, M.D., Department of Child Psychiatry, Harlem Hospital Center, New York; Rabbi Jacob Goldberg, Rabbinical Bereavement Counseling Program of the New York Board of Rabbis; Janet Kamien, Boston Children's Museum; Elliot Kranzier, M.D., Department of Child Psychiatry, Columbia University College of Physicians and Surgeons, New York; Austin H. Kutscher, President, Foundation of Thanatology, Columbia University College of Physicians and Surgeons; Harriet Lainer; Leonard Levy; Richard Lonetto, Ph.D.; Otto S. Margolis, Ph.D., American Academy McAllister Institute of Funeral Services; Susan McCormick; the Reverend Luciano Padilla, Jr., Bay Ridge Christian Center, New York; David Peretz, M.D., Department of Psychiatry, Columbia University College of Physicians and Surgeons; Gwen Schwartz-Borden, C.S.W., Family Service Association, Nassau County, New York; the Reverend Mark Wilhelm, Bethany Lutheran Church, Brooklyn, New York.

In addition, I would especially like to thank the families I have assisted, whose confidence, trust, sharing, and encouragement have made this book possible. — D. S.

Thanks to William Cole, Anne Crosman, Irving Danker, Jack Kennington, C.S.S.R., and Simon Perchik for their kindness and help. — C. L.

Special thanks to our publisher, Esther Margolis, our agent, Felicia Eth, and our editor, Katherine Heintzelman, who helped craft a complicated topic.

# Contents

Preface by Dan Schaefer, Ph.D.                                          xi

Foreword by David Peretz, M.D.                                          xiii

Introduction: The Solitary Mourner                                      1

1. What Children Think About Death                                      11

    TWO TO SIX YEARS                              16

    SIX TO NINE YEARS                             20

    NINE TO TWELVE YEARS                          21

    TEENAGERS                                     24

2. Explaining Death to Children                                         26

    DEATH OF A GRANDPARENT                        27

    DEATH OF AN IMMEDIATE FAMILY MEMBER

        (MOTHER, FATHER, SIBLING)                 41

    INFANT DEATH                                  47

    DEATH OF A FRIEND OR CLASSMATE                55

    ACCIDENTAL DEATH                              58

    MURDER                                        59

    SUICIDE                                       62

    AIDS                                          70

    HOW TO TALK TO CHILDREN ABOUT

        SOMEONE WHO IS DYING                      79

HOW TO TALK TO A MENTALLY

    RETARDED CHILD                                      91

DEATH OF A PET                                             93


3. Grief and Healing                                       95

COMMON REACTIONS TO GRIEF                                   98

THE SPECIAL NEEDS OF CHILDREN                              103

THE GRIEVING PROCESS                                       106

PROBLEMS TO BE PREPARED FOR AT

    VARIOUS AGES                                       112

DEALING WITH ANGER, GUILT, AND

    RESPONSIBILITY                                     119

HELPING YOUR CHILD TO HEAL                                 124


4. Expectations for the Grieving Child and the

  Best Ways to Respond                                   131

TRAUMATIC STRESS                                           139

ONE PERSONAL EXPERIENCE OF TRAUMA

    BY DR. LISA HUDSON                                 144

SCHOOLS AND TRAUMA                                         155


5. The Funeral—Finding a Way to Say Good-bye               158

TELLING CHILDREN WHAT TO EXPECT                            161

A GOOD-BYE GIFT                                            165

QUESTIONS YOUR CHILD MIGHT ASK                             167


"Life Goes On" by Pat Travis Rosenberg                     169

Crisis Checklist                                           171

Bibliography and Support Groups                            187

Index                                                      197

About the Authors                                          203

# Preface:
# by Dan Schaefer, Ph.D.

As the third edition of *How Do We Tell the Children?* goes to press after a year in editorial development, our nation has just sustained the most devastating terrorist attack in its history.

The destruction of the World Trade Center towers in New York City, the attack on the Pentagon in Washington, D.C., and the crashing of four commercial airliners that were used in the hijackings took the lives of many thousands of innocent civilians and military personnel, including hundreds of firefighters, police, and rescue workers who came to their aid.

The loss of life is almost beyond our ability to comprehend. The impact of this traumatic event on surviving families, friends, co-workers, rescue workers, and those who witnessed the events around the world is beyond calculation.

It is my sincere hope that the information contained in this edition, with a new section specifically directed toward traumatic loss, will help us all create a nurturing environment where those affected may heal.

I, along with my friends and colleagues, whose personal

experiences and research in the area of traumatic loss made this edition possible, offer our prayers for the victims, their survivors, and all those whose listening and caring will make healing possible.

—DAN SCHAEFER, PH.D.

# Foreword
# by David Peretz, M.D.

---

Many years ago, I heard Dan Schaefer speak to an audience
of health professionals and educators concerned with dying,
death, and bereavement. His point of view had developed as
an outgrowth of meeting with bereaved families in their
acute grief in the funeral setting. His presentation was remarkable for its sensitivity, openness, and simplicity. Here
was a man who was totally committed to helping families in
a time of terrible stress, and who had the gift of caring about
the most vulnerable members of the family—the children.

Dan's work with families in acute grief convinced him
that children were often either gently shunted aside,
avoided, or misinformed with "cover stories" by bereaved
parents, relatives, and friends. Many bereaved adults find
the effort of listening to their children and communicating
with them openly about their loss and grief almost more
than they can bear. This is intensified by fears of hurting or
upsetting the child, saying or doing something wrong. They
are not aware that it could be more harmful to avoid the
subject, to "protect" the child from the facts of death, than
to deal with them in a simple, straightforward manner. Dan
Schaefer gradually realized the pernicious short- and
long-term effects that such avoidance, neglect, and misin-

formation could have upon children. And like the pioneer he is, he set out to do something about the problem. The funeral chapel was his setting, and his generous heart and inquiring mind his research instruments. His added strength lay in his straightforwardness. He was unencumbered by professional jargon or theories about human behavior. He began, as most outstanding clinicians begin, with simple observation.

Meeting with hundreds, and ultimately thousands, of parents and their children provided him with a broad range of experience. He talked to toddlers and preschoolers, young children and adolescents, and found each of them likely to have specific concerns based on their relationship to the person who had died and on their dependency needs, according to age and circumstance. He learned that there are patterns of thought and imagination common to children at particular stages in their development, and that these patterns are reflected in the kinds of questions children ask.

On the basis of these conversations, observations, and experiences, Dan worked out a common sense approach to talking with children about death. He checked it out with educators, psychologists, psychiatrists, clergy, and other professionals who had formed a new discipline—that of thanatology, the study of dying, death, and bereavement. Dan found a good fit between what these professionals knew about children's needs and what he had discovered as approaches to those needs. I had been working in thanatology since 1966, and when I heard Dan's presentation of his approach in 1982, I said to myself, "Here's an original." I went up to Dan at the conclusion of the presentations, congratulated him, and said, "You've got to write a book!" He looked at me, a little startled, and replied, "I've been thinking about it." When he called me two years later to tell me that he was, in fact, working on the book, I was delighted. I am even more delighted with the end result of that labor.

It is my belief that children thrive in a climate of realism: realistic limits, realistic demands made upon them in tune with their growing capacities, and realistic answers to their questions, pitched to the level of their understanding. This can best be provided in an atmosphere where parents listen respectfully to their children. Genuine listening requires being prepared to make new discoveries and to share sorrow and fear. This is difficult at any time; it is most difficult when the parent is in grief.

The very young approach life as naturalists, open-minded and curious. Unfortunately, their early experiences with death and the reactions of those around them frequently close down their openness and curiosity, leading to avoidance and denial. A child's first questions about death are an attempt to gain mastery over frightening images of abandonment, separation, loneliness, pain, and bodily damage. If we err on the side of overprotecting them from emotional pain and grief with "kind" lies, we risk weakening their coping capacities. Children will absorb our defensiveness, avoidance, denial, and general unwillingness to discuss death directly. Death becomes, quite literally, something unspeakable.

*How Do We Tell the Children?* makes it clear that when children are confronted with death or ask questions about it, they can and should be informed, simply and honestly and without overelaboration. With an eloquent simplicity, it demonstrates how parents can deal with their children's concepts, as well as their questions. If we are to encourage the growth of realistic thinking in our children, if we are to help them overcome the fear of death as violent and mutilating, we must engage in a dialogue with them. A parent's voice and image, valued and respected by the child, discussing death in a simple and honest way, is internalised for a lifetime as a source of strength and comfort in facing loss and grief. This book will, I believe, help parents find their voice to speak to their children. In so doing, they will be giving their children an invaluable gift.

## Addendum: October 2001

Dan Schaefer went on to earn his Ph.D. and to gain international recognition for his pioneering efforts in assisting individuals in acute grief as well as corporations in their efforts to reduce the impact of loss and life transition in the workplace. As always, Dan Schaefer learns while contributing in each new setting in which he serves, whether it is an educational institution, Survivors of the Shield, or TAPS, an organization caring for the survivors of military loss. The reader is the beneficiary of his learning and his remarkable ability to communicate simply, clearly, and directly. This third edition of *How Do We Tell the Children?* could not be more timely, given the terrible events of September 11th. The landscape in which many of us now live is transformed compelling us to deal not only with loss and grief, but with traumatic stress. The invaluable material in this edition has been enriched with new material, specifically on trauma and loss. Colleagues and patients to whom I have recommended the book over the years have found it invaluable. The book has stood the test of time and should be read not only by parents, but by grandparents, teachers, guidance councilors, physicians, nurses, social workers, and mental health professionals in every field.

DAVID PERETZ, M.D.
Department of Psychiatry, Columbia University College
of Physicians and Surgeons Faculty, Columbia University
Psychoanalytic Center for Training and Research
Chairperson, Advisory Board,
American Institute for Life-Threatening Illness and Loss

# Introduction:
# The Solitary Mourner

On any day around four o'clock you could set your watch by them—Michael and his grandfather, walking down the street, hand in hand, to the corner store. Michael and Grandpa, the young and the old—best friends. They shared a two-family house in an outlying section of New York City; the old man lived upstairs, Michael and his parents downstairs. It had been that way since the child was born. When Michael was about seven, his family moved to Long Island, leaving Grandpa back in the city. "See you on Thanksgiving!" they all said. Thanksgiving came and went; no Grandpa. Same with Christmas. "Grandpa's away for a while," Michael's parents explained. "Don't worry about it." Months went by and the child waited. Finally, when his birthday came and Grandpa didn't even send a card, Michael knew something was up. What could he have done to make Grandpa not love him anymore?

It was two years before Michael's parents told him what had really happened—that his grandfather had died shortly

1

after they moved to Long Island. "I know they thought they were doing the right thing," Michael says now. "But it was a terrible time for me. They certainly didn't spare me any pain while I was wondering what had happened. And then when they finally told me the truth, I still had to deal with the feeling of losing Grandpa."

Whenever someone close to the family dies, each and every member of that family is affected. For the first few days, many parents have told me, they felt numb and drained by their grief, as though someone had pulled the plug and sucked all the energy out of them. It's an overwhelming, stressful time, and there are so many details to attend to—funeral arrangements to be made, relatives to be notified. And all of this when you feel like a videotape running in slow motion, out of synch. For many people, the support they receive during this difficult period is crucial, helping them hold their world together. Neighbors stop by and bring in food. Relatives gather and minister to each other, sometimes after years of being separated. People cry and reminisce and comfort each other in their loss, and grief is allowed to flow.

Very often, though, the children in the family are shut out of this support network, given inaccurate or incomplete information, and not included in the activities that can be such a necessary part of coping with a death. The fortunate ones, whom the network does support and nurture, are what I call "inside kids"; those, like Michael, whom the network ignores are "outside kids." "Outside kids" feel abandoned, lonely, angry, and confused.

This came home to me for the first time about nine years ago. I was sitting in the office of my family funeral home in Brooklyn when a nine-year-old boy walked in. "My uncle out there," he said, pointing to the viewing room, "Why did he die?" I was really taken aback. "I think you'd better talk to your parents about that," I said. But as I sat there watching him walk out, I was filled with sympathy for the child. No one had told him what had happened. I realized that his parents probably didn't know what to say, and I thought—how alone that boy must feel!

I've worked with more than 3,000 parents during the days just after a death, and one thing I know for sure—many people find it almost impossible to talk with their children about death. "How do we tell the children?" they ask. "I can talk to them about sex or drinking or drugs . . . just about anything. But when it comes to talking about death, forget it."

There are a number of reasons for this. First, there's the philosophy "Let kids be kids." Parents tell me that they don't want to worry their children with problems, that they'll have enough to worry about when they get older; that their children are too young to understand and that, before you know it, they'll forget that the person even existed.

Many parents opt not to deal with the situation because they don't want to put their children or themselves through unnecessary pain. As Jeannie said several days after her father's funeral, "I simply couldn't bear to watch my little Evan crying and talking about how much he missed his grandpa. And I didn't want my mother to have to go through that either. It's my own feelings I'm trying to protect. I know that. But I just can't handle it right now."

Children say what they think and feel, honestly and openly, and in their directness our protection is stripped away. They say things that force us to confront the loss straight on, to deal with the emotional reality of a situation. When someone dies we're suddenly confronted with our own mortality, something that we never talk about, something that most of us are afraid to think about.

Andrew comes from a very close family that believes in sheltering children from the unpleasant things in life. When he was about six, his cousin, whom he often played with, all of a sudden disappeared. "Don't worry," said one of the relatives, "he'll come back some day." Andrew remembers waiting and waiting for his cousin, wondering when he'd be coming back. Several years later, he realized that his little friend had died. "They weren't really trying to lie to me," Andrew says now, looking back on that time. "Their story was partially true, because our family believes that at the end of the world everyone does come back. They were just using a gimmick to try to help me."

Helping young people cope better is what we're all interested in. But avoiding the issue or making up fairy tales to explain away death are devices that almost always fall apart. Saying Grandpa's away on a camping trip while all the relatives are moving in and out of the house in various stages of grief is a charade that the youngster will soon get wise to. Even a three-year-old will sense that something is happening. Children know when we're bothered or afraid to talk about something. They pick up the unspoken vibrations that all is not well. The mood of the house has a certain cadence to it, a certain rhythm. Every day your child gets a consistent message that things go along and that people act in a certain way. Then one day all that changes.

Jimmy's mother sat in my office making arrangements for her husband's funeral.

"What have you said to your children?" I asked her.

"The two oldest know their father died. I don't think I'll tell the little guy."

"Is he at home right now?"

"Yes."

"Are the bigger kids all upset?"

"Of course."

"What do you think little Jimmy thinks is going on?"

"He keeps asking about his daddy."

"What do you say?"

"I tell him he's still very sick."

"Is everyone acting the same way they did when he was sick?"

"No, the older ones are really upset. . . . Do you think the little guy knows?"

Certainly, an adult is better equipped than a child to cope with a death in the family. Armed with years of experience that help cushion the blow, adults are also privy to the facts—what really happened, what's going to happen. That knowledge and experience give us comfort in our loss. We've been through painful times and we know they don't last forever.

Children, on the other hand, have no idea what to expect when death and grief are concerned. If they have not been given an explanation of what happened—or if they can't believe or understand the explanation they have been given— they will use what little information they can get to construct their own notion of why the people around them are so upset. Very often, a youngster creates a wild fantasy, which is actually much worse than the harsh reality of death. Thought to be not mature enough to handle the bad news, the child is often given partial or distorted information. But if he's been given an inadequate explanation, he'll sense a cover-up and become frightened by the unknown. "Something bad happened," he might think to himself. "What did I do? Maybe everyone's upset because I wet my bed last week!"

That's what happened with Jerry when he was a youngster. Now in his mid-twenties, he says he remembers his grandmother's death as clearly as if it were yesterday.

> "My grandmother was ill at home, and the family was all around her when she died. I was immediately taken across the street to a neighbor's house, never allowed to see Grandmother, to be with the others, or to go to the funeral. I remember running and hiding under the bed after they left. I couldn't understand why I had to be alone while everyone else was together somewhere else. I kept thinking that since they wouldn't let me come to see her, how horrible she must look! Nobody told me what was going on. It took a long time before I could forgive my parents."

Another man I talked with, a middle-aged rabbi whose father died when he was seven, still remembers the family gathered in the living room, wailing. "I didn't know what it meant. I was so alone and afraid. And for years I used to have daydreams that my father would come back."

Psychiatrist Bruce Danto of Fullerton, California, says that keeping a child in the dark when there's a death can be humiliating to a youngster. "The way it comes across to the child is, 'Look, kid, you bother me. You're in the way. You're not entitled to know what's going on here.'"

When this happens, the child is put in the position of being a "solitary mourner." One of the saddest things to see is a casket in a church or funeral home with just one mourner beside it. I've actually seen people drop into church for a quick visit, then change their plans and stay for the funeral when they see someone they don't even know sitting up front alone by a casket. No one wants to let a person grieve alone. And yet this is what happens to many children, in effect, when someone they have been close to dies.

A final reason that we find it so difficult to talk to our children about death is that we just don't know what to say. We're not very comfortable with the idea of death ourselves, and we often use euphemisms to hide our discomfort. We're especially unprepared to discuss it in terms that children can understand, and to answer the myriad questions that children always have.

A child's mind does not work the same way as an adult's. Less sophisticated, it processes information about subjects like death differently. This sounds obvious, but it's easy to forget. One parent said to me recently, "I told Valerie, 'Your cousin died,' that's all. She knows what that means." But does she? Does she know what "dead" means? Does she know why the person died, and what's going to happen to the body? These sorts of questions are on the minds of most children who are faced with a death, and they need answers.

Although death is still treated by many as a taboo subject, when Will Lee, the actor who played Dr. Hooper on TV's "Sesame Street," died several years ago, the show's producers took the opportunity to explain the death to their young viewers. "We felt we ought to deal with it head-on. If we left it unsaid, the kids would notice," producer Dulcy Singer explained in an interview at the time. "Our instincts told us to be honest and straightforward." After consulting with a child psychologist, the "Sesame Street" writers prepared a script designed to answer some basic questions a preschooler would have. "Who's going to take care of the store?" asks Big Bird, the show's representative five-year-old. "Who's going to make me birdseed milkshakes and tell me stories?" David, the neighborhood's father, answers, "We'll all tell you stories and make sure you're okay." "It won't be the same," says the grieving Big Bird.

Susan seemed to be a textbook example of how to handle

children when someone close to them dies. When her husband was killed, she kept her cool and pulled her children
in close to her. A very down-to-earth, sensible woman, she
gave the straight story to any questions the children asked,
explaining what had happened to their father, including
them in the wake and funeral, and telling them if they had
any further questions, they should ask—she'd explain what
she could. But after a few months went by, Susan realized
that she was missing some important information. "It wasn't
enough to just explain how their father died," she told me.
"I had to learn to help them cope with their feelings of loss,
and I had no way of knowing what was going on in their
heads."

Susan was prepared with the right attitude for marvelous
parent-child communication. By instinct, she knew part of
the message she needed to send—openness, honesty, the
freedom to ask questions, and to grieve. But she was lacking
a lot of the information we'll give you in this book—how to
talk with children of all ages about death; what they think
and understand; how they feel, and how you can help them
cope with their feelings.

The program outlined in this book grew out of my personal experience with thousands of families who have come
to my funeral home, as well as consultations with psychologists, social workers, and other professionals. It is also based
on lectures I've given at workshops and symposia dealing
with children and grief. The book is divided into chapters
that will tell you what children aged two and up already
know and are capable of understanding about death; what
words to use when explaining death, including special situations such as accident and illness; and how to help your
child deal with grief. In addition, there is a special Crisis
Checklist at the back of the book that distills much of this

information into a ready reference guide. This program has worked for a lot of different people in a lot of different circumstances. You may not relate to everything in this book, but I think you'll find that much of it will help.

Unlike other parenting guides, where if you look at the picture long enough you'll eventually learn how to change a diaper, you'll have to take the information I give you and tailor it to your own situation. But you won't be going it alone—you'll be part of a large group of parents who have broken the communication barrier and helped their children feel more at ease talking about death and the complex mix of emotions that surround it.

# 1

## What Children Think About Death

To communicate with children effectively, we have to know what they're thinking—what's going in their minds. As communicators, it's our responsibility to package our message so that children will not only listen but understand what we're trying to tell them. Before we can structure what we're going to say, we have to appreciate the child's level of development and what he or she already knows about death. The message to a four-year-old will obviously be very different from one we'd give to a teenager, but in both cases it must be finely tuned, gently presented, and double-checked so that we're sure that the child got the story straight. If we package the message well, it will make things a lot easier on both ourselves and our children during a time of crisis. We parents will be giving our children the information they need, and our children will trust what we're saying.

One thing children *don't* need is to be loaded down with all the scientific information and explicit details about how the person died . . . at least not at the beginning. A simple explanation is what you're aiming for. Assessing the situation, looking at the age and maturity of the child, will help determine how much he or she can handle.

In this chapter we'll show you how to do that by giving some guidelines on the ways children think at different ages. You decide what best fits your child, and then you'll be able to construct the right message for him or her.

A child's thinking is very much influenced by his surroundings, colored by what he sees and hears. Consider what the average youngster views on TV. The coyote chasing roadrunner gets mashed, maimed, and flattened, only to pop up and start racing around again. Hundreds of people die each year on the news programs. The cops-and-robbers shows do away with several bad guys per night. Children even act out death as they're playing: "Bang, bang, you're dead!" Some parents, when the suggestion is made that they talk to their children about death, protest that they don't want to expose them to such a difficult thing. And yet children are absorbing death all the time! Just as we can't follow them around protecting them for the rest of their lives, so we can't shelter them from the idea of death.

Given the fact that the youngster knows there is such a thing as death, what does he or she understand about this particular death facing you now? Did he or she know the person was sick? Was there a lingering illness, or a sudden heart attack? For an adult who watched Grandpa slowly deteriorate, the experience had a continuity—sick, sicker, sickest—and the death was not unexpected. But for a child who didn't know how sick Grandpa was, that death had the shocking effect of a sudden tragedy. If the child has been given straightforward reports—Grandpa's getting worse, he's not getting better, he may die—he or she will be a bit more prepared when the crisis comes.

Did the child know Grandpa was old? For a youngster, whose frame of reference is different from that of an adult, Mommy and Daddy are very old.

Was Grandpa killed in an accident? What happened? What kind of information does the child have about how the death occurred? Those parents who just say "He died" leave a lot to the child's imagination. What might other people have told him about what happened? And what might he have overheard? One woman I know, who was nine when her mother died, remembers lying in her bedroom listening to the grownups whispering in the living room. One of her friends had told her that a poisonous smell had killed her mother. And so she lay there imagining that she too was dying, and the relatives were whispering, afraid to tell her.

"Whispers are terrible to a child," says child psychiatrist Hal Fishkin, who works with bereaved children in New York City. "Whispers, secrets, fairy tales. . . . It's really patronizing to assume children can't deal with the traumas we can. Having experienced some major losses without data in my own life, I can tell you it's a rather mind-maiming experience. It makes you come up with conclusions in your own little head that are not consonant with reality, and you always come up on the short end of the stick. Something terrible has happened and it's all your fault. The fantasy is always worse than the reality."

One way to find out just what your youngsters are thinking is by listening to them explain what has happened to another child. "Grandma's walking the earth," one seven-year-old told another, obviously very upset about possibly having the ghost drop in for a visit. Where did she ever get such an idea? The mother finally found out that in religion class the child had heard something about spirits walking the earth. The little girl put that together with the opening on a TV show that shows a man sitting up in a casket, and she had the makings of a wild and scary misconception about death. Fortunately, her mother overheard that conversation, and she gave the child the facts and eased her mind. "That only happens in the movies. It's make-believe—just like Superman flying."

Sometimes as I explain my program to people they point out that I'm talking like a child. Well, that's just the point. You don't speak in German if you're talking to a Frenchman. You have to stoop down or put the child on your lap, look into his eyes, and talk to him in his language—but never in a condescending way. Listen to your child carefully and sympathetically, as you would to a good friend going through a crisis.

Go beyond the words and listen with your heart. Dr. Hal Fishkin says that "forcing yourself to walk in his moccasins will yield the right way to go when you're trying to talk with a child. Find out what he knows and what he's experienced, and you can pretty well guess what some of his ideas and feelings are."

In my own experience working with children and their parents, I've found that although each child is, of course, a unique individual, there are certain things you can predict that most children will say. A child of a certain age thinks in a certain way; this is not true of all of them, of course, but it's true enough for us to make some generalizations. One of these generalizations is that children think about and are concerned about death.

In *How It Feels to Be a Child*, Carole Klein points out that studies show a high percentage of children (80 percent) think about death. They wrestle with fears about it without telling their parents, burying their thoughts and feelings inside, just as their parents do. That's surprising to many adults, who assume that if a child doesn't talk about something he or she is not thinking about it. Not long ago I had the following conversation with seven-year-old Leon.

> "My grandma died last year," Leon said to me.
>
> "Oh, it must have been very hard for you. Were you close?"
>
> "Yes, she lived with us since I was a baby and took care of me when Mommy went to work."
>
> "You must have had a lot of fun with Grandma."
>
> "Sure. She used to read to me a lot. We had a lot of fun."
>
> "Did you tell anyone you missed her?" I asked.
>
> "Well, every time I talked about Grandma everyone would cry. So I stopped. . . ."
>
> "Do you think a lot about dying?"
>
> "Yes, but not me dying."
>
> "Well, who?"
>
> "My parents. I'm afraid a lot. I don't like Mommy and Daddy to go out without me."
>
> "Have you ever told anyone?"
>
> "Only you. Nobody wants to talk to me about it."

Remember that a child usually builds his whole world around his mother and father. They are the ones who take care of him, feed him, hug him, protect him. A very young child can grasp only what he sees, his known world. If you talk to him about dying, of someone going away and not coming back, his mind frequently turns to his parents, and he becomes afraid that they too are going to die.

Very often when a child hears something he misunderstands what is being said. Then, to complicate matters, when he can't understand something or doesn't have enough information to bring his ideas to a logical conclusion, he often makes up the part of the message that's missing. With lack of information, his reasoning becomes twisted.

Psychiatrist Bruce Danto points out that children sometimes get some pretty strange ideas just by watching things happen around them. "The thing that children will notice is that somebody doesn't look well . . . that 'Grandpa's not playing with me. Why is Grandpa so pale?' " Now if Grandpa is at home, getting intravenous feeding, and it's not explained to the children that those tubes are there to help put medicine into Grandpa, the young child can be very frightened. "That's not my Grandpa who used to be around here. That's Grandpa the monster!"

As I said, there are certain ways of thinking and acting that are unique to children at various stages of development. While many of the characteristics overlap, there are four distinct groups and levels of development: two- to six-year-olds; six- to nine-year-olds; nine- to twelve-year-olds; and teenagers.

## TWO TO SIX YEARS

Stop for a moment and watch a preschooler at play. To him or her the world is a magical place, full of people coming and going around the family, the center of the world. It's a world in transition, a time of learning and growing and finding out how things work. Concepts like time and death are not yet fully developed in the preschooler's mind; he simply can't grasp them. What he can understand are the day-to-day things in life, and the feeling of his family taking care of him.

Since a young child's experience and vocabulary are limited, he has to draw on what he knows. Imitating the world around him, she picks up Mommy's pocketbook or he puts on Daddy's shoes, trying to see how a grownup feels. "I'm going to work now!" the child asserts, mimicking a parent as he or she shuffles down the hall.

Young children are equally sensitive to our nonverbal attitudes. If we are reserved, fearful, suspicious, or hostile, very often our children will pick up on those feelings and act just like us. If we are open, honest, warm, and loving, they will get the message that that's the way to be.

Children in this age group generally do not think of death as final; to them, *death is reversible*. In order to understand the finality of death, a youngster has to recognize that he is a separate person from his parents — that without them he can still exist. While older children can comprehend this, most preschoolers cannot. They are helpless by themselves, dependent, and they know they need to be protected. A world without his parents is beyond his grasp. His mind also can't imagine the nothingness of death. So, if he hears that someone dies, he figures it's a temporary thing — you die and then come back; it's like going out to the grocery store. Just as characters on TV disappear on one show and appear on another, so will Grandpa rise from the dead. He's dead only for a little time. He's still eating and moving around; it's just that he now happens to be underground or up in the sky somewhere. Whatever Grandpa happened to be doing when we last saw him, he's still doing it now.

One little fellow, Roy, age five, was on his first airplane trip when he asked his mother to open the window. "I want to give JoJo some dinner," he explained. Roy's thinking was that the plane was flying around heaven and that his friend JoJo, who had died a few months before, was hiding behind one of the clouds, alive and well and hungry. His sister Fredericka, just a year older, described how JoJo got up to heaven: "The angels came down and got JoJo, and like E.T.

she rose up into heaven one night. There had to be a whole bunch of angels to hold her because JoJo was so big."

*Magical thinking* plays a big role in children's lives at this age, and of course it extends to their thoughts about death. Some young children, for example, imagine that by putting a body in water, you'll bring it back to life, like a dehydrated food. Others figure that if they wish hard enough they can bring the dead person back to life.

Sometimes they even invest themselves with magical powers. "I'll go beat up the bad man who killed Auntie!" The child in his imagination fashions a set of powers that counters all the disquieting facts he's seen around him.

It's partly because of the magical world they create that youngsters get the courage to deal with the problems of life; but sometimes they go a little overboard. Consider the little girl who was playing in her grandmother's yard, bouncing the ball against the wall, over and over. In exasperation the grandmother yelled, "Stop doing that! You'll be the death of me yet!" The child thought about that for a moment, then started playing something else. A few days later Grandma died. "Boy, I've done it now!" The child thought she had killed her grandmother.

*Connecting events* that don't belong together is something children commonly do that many adults find hard to understand. In the example I just gave, the little girl connected the bouncing ball incident and the death of her grandmother, which filled her with guilt and a feeling of responsibility. Since most youngsters have a hard time admitting that they threw the ball that broke a window, you can imagine how hard it would be to tell someone that she killed her grandmother! That's why it's important to get to her and explain what really happened to Grandma before she distorts the incident out of all proportion in her mind.

Adults seldom make these kinds of connections because their reasoning powers are developed. But children who are searching for a beginning, middle, and end to a story will fill in the blanks and simply make up a message when they're missing the facts.

They also take the admonitions of adults quite literally. "You have to eat so your body will get big and strong." That's what four-year-old Tim was told as he made soup out of his mashed potatoes one evening. The next morning his father died. Strange as it may seem, the child thought he had killed his father by not eating his potatoes. In another instance, Jimmy overheard Aunt Millie saying that Grandpa had died in his sleep. "Thank God, it was so peaceful. He just fell asleep and died." When it came time for Jimmy to go to bed that night he wanted no part of it; he was afraid that he wouldn't wake up either.

A child hears that Grandpa got sick and died, and the next time Daddy starts to cough or the child himself gets a stomach pain, watch his reaction. "What color shirt was Grandpa wearing when he died?" he might ask. Tell him a blue one (without explaining that it had nothing to do with Grandpa's death), then see what happens the next time you try to put his blue pullover on him.

One middle-aged friend of mine, who has more gray hairs than he would like, could not understand why his grandson clung to him so tightly. He asked the child what was the matter. The reply: "You're very old, too [the gray hair], and I don't want you to die!"

Another little boy, named Brett, overheard that his grandfather had looked awful for the past few weeks, and he filed that away. A week later the child was watching a Saturday afternoon monster movie, in which some humanoid was melting across the screen. His mother came in and said,

"Oh, I can't let you watch that. That's awful-looking!" and she switched off the TV. "Aha!" said the child to himself, and his mind connected three events. Here's how the syllogism went in his mind: 1) Grandpa looked awful; he died, and Mommy wouldn't let me go to see him; 2) That humanoid looked awful, and Mommy wouldn't let me watch him on TV; 3) Grandpa must look as horrible as that monster on TV. And that's the final picture the youngster retained of the grandfather he loved so much.

For parents to help their children, they must be aware that things like this may be going on in their heads. The experience of death is probably new and strange to them, and their feelings of confusion and guilt when someone they were close to dies may be absolutely overwhelming.

## SIX TO NINE YEARS

Children who are around the ages of six to nine often look on death as a taker, something violent that comes and gets you, like a burglar or a ghost. When they hear that someone died, these children may ask, "Who killed him?" In their minds death is personified, an external agent that catches you. It's a scary skeleton or a bogeyman to be run away from or to be handled by magic.

Although children in this age group have begun to comprehend the finality of death, very often they retain a lot of that magical thinking, overestimating the power of their thoughts and wishes. They may accept the fact that someone has died and that it's final, but they don't accept the fact that it must happen to everyone, especially themselves.

Many children of this age are afraid that death is *contagious*, something that can be caught, like a cold. Some even think that if another child's parent dies they can catch death by playing with that child, or by playing in the house where the dead person lived. Little phrases and chants that they hear can have a traumatic effect on them. There was a popular bedtime verse: "Now I lay me down to sleep, I pray the Lord my soul to keep; if I should die before I wake, I pray the Lord my soul to take." It caused many youngsters to worry about dying in their sleep. To get that fantasy material that is so scary to them out where we can help them deal with it, we have to get them to talk about it.

Still in a transitional stage, children aged six to nine find many words confusing. Some words have several meanings, and often the child can't differentiate between them. Take the word "soul," for example. One researcher told the story of a child caught in a fantasy who thought he heard his dead father speaking to him from a shoe box in the closet. In the child's mind, "soul" and the "sole" of a shoe had become all mixed up.

## NINE TO TWELVE YEARS

As a child grows in the nine-to-twelve age group, he or she develops an acute sense of morality, of right and wrong behavior. Very often children will think of death as a *punishment* for bad behavior; an unkind person's death was due to his wrongdoing. Though they're making the transition to a more adult understanding of the concept of death, they will sometimes have remnants of magical thinking and the "I did it" syndrome. The child who resisted going to see his grandmother when she was sick, thinking, "Why do I have to go to see her? I'm missing my ball game. If only she wasn't around!" may be plagued with guilt when she dies. He probably wouldn't admit it to anyone, and it would take some detective work to find out that that's what he's thinking—but it's important to children to know that wishes don't kill. You might start out by saying, "Some children think that a person can die if you just think about their dying," and see how your child responds.

At this age children will probably be interested in the biological details of what happened. Unlike younger children, they have a frame of reference now and can handle much of the information you would give an adult. Because of their schooling in science, some preteens understand more about the biology and chemistry of the body than we adults do.

Because they are experimenting with ideas and theories, they may think that death is a way of getting rid of people, to make ready for new ones. Another theory you hear among children in these "middle years" is that each time there's a death, there's a birth.

Their cognitive and emotional skills are in transition, and children this age have standards and concerns that are very important to them, such as the idea that when something dies it should be buried. Preteens often handle the funeral of a pet with great ceremony and ritual. Elaine, a twelve-year-old whose guinea pig died, seemed to express the same degree of concern for the burial of her pet as another child did for her father who had died six months earlier. Elaine was quite concerned about all the details—that it be buried in the "right place" in the yard, that the shoe box it was being buried in was clean, and so on.

Children in this age group have usually gone beyond wondering what death is. They're more caught up in questions of relationship. "Grandpa won't be able to go fishing with me anymore." "Who's going to take care of Grandma now?" "What's going to happen to our family now that he has died?" Concerned with practical things, the child wonders if the family's style of life will change; who will run the house, or make the money.

> "Why did you put all those good clothes on my father? It's a terrible waste of money."
>
> "Why is that?"
>
> "Well, all the dirt's going to get on him when he's buried."
>
> "You know, we close the casket before it's buried."
>
> "Oh, I didn't know that."

You might have thought that a preadolescent would know that when a casket is put in the ground the top is closed. But you can't assume that a child knows the same things as an adult. Also, in a stressful situation surrounding a death, children who might otherwise be very mature in their thinking may regress to an earlier stage of emotional response.

None of these stages that we are talking about is set in stone. Children move back and forth among them. Child psychiatrist Hal Fishkin thinks this process continues all the way through adulthood—that we are never entirely out of one stage and into another. "I think if you scratch most of the people you know, myself included, you'll find a residue of magical thinking. And when it comes to death, you'll have children who, because of the better education today, seem to be very mature, who know more about death, but who respond emotionally in a very infantile way. It's up to the parents to find out how their children think and how they communicate. And the only way they can do this is to ask them. So, if you give a little educational sermon on death, I would suggest that you ask the kids questions on what you've just told them to make sure they've got it straight."

## TEENAGERS

By the time children are in their teens, they probably understand just as well as adults what happens when a person dies. Unlike the younger child, they see death as something universal, inevitable, and irreversible. Acutely aware of themselves as people, teenagers may spend a lot of time philosophizing, criticizing, and daydreaming.

With puberty they watch their bodies change and mature, seeing the natural progression of the aging process that makes death possible. Death is a natural enemy to this new self who's emerging. If a person grows up to die, what's the sense of life? they ask.

With very young children, we have to spend a lot of time thinking about the words to use to help them understand about death. With a teen this usually isn't necessary. But what *is* necessary when they are confronted with death is to be there to help them through their grief, to understand their emotions, and to teach them how to act in this crisis. In this time of flux when they're shifting from being dependent to being independent, and experimenting with values and ways of behaving, teenagers need some firm and gentle guidance, someone to talk to. They are probably concerned about where they fit in at this time, what they're expected to do, and how to handle the myriad emotions that are brewing inside them. They may be feeling guilt, responsibility, and anger. "If only I had bugged Grandpa to take his medicine." "If only I had gone to see him in the hospital." They probably also have a heightened awareness of their parents' vulnerability. It all of a sudden hits them that nobody lives forever . . . how transient life is.

In her book *Peoplemaking*, Virginia Satir points out that parents teach in the toughest school in the world: the school of making people. In order to help them grow into kind, stable adults, we need to listen to them, talk with them, guide them. We have to treat them like people.

As we've seen, children are people with a special way of seeing the world. They have unusual ideas about death, and they are prone to certain misconceptions and difficulties with the subject at different ages. However, children can understand almost anything if it's put to them in the right way. You just have to know the right words to say. We'll talk more about this in the next chapter.

# 2

## Explaining Death to Children

A six-year-old walked into the office of a funeral director in New Jersey, circled around the desk, and asked my colleague, "Mister, where are your wings?" The astonished man asked what the youngster meant and the child replied, "Well, Mommy said that an angel was coming to take Grandpa to heaven."

No one was trying to deceive that child. His mother was just giving him the best information she had at the time. The problem was that she hadn't packaged her message well, and on the way from parent to child the transmission was garbled. She hadn't used the right words to make the child understand what happens when a person dies.

Each family dealing with a death has a special set of circumstances unique to itself, depending on the individuals involved, their cultural traditions, religious beliefs, and what the children in the family know about death. All of these factors go into making up a sort of *family blueprint*, a way that each family has of doing things. No two family blueprints are the same, and in this book, no one explanation that I offer will be exactly right for everyone, or will fit precisely into each family's blueprint. A family with a 95-year-old aunt who has just died of old age won't have the same frame of reference as one in which a child died in an automobile accident. The family that has had to cope with two deaths in the last four years has a very different set of experiences than one that has never before experienced a death. There are no pat answers. What is right for Family A may not apply to Family B or C.

Look at your own family blueprint and see what it's made of. Who is the person who died? A distant relative, a grandparent you saw on weekends, or a member of the immediate family? How close that person was to the children will determine how deeply they will be affected.

I expect you to pick and choose from the information provided here. If you have a five-year-old, you may want to disregard the sections dealing with teenagers, taking only the information you need right now. First I'll talk about death close to home, in the family, then I'll discuss death outside the home—in the classroom, for example. Finally, we'll take a look at special situations that might come up— the death of an infant, accidental death, and the violent deaths of murder and suicide. In each case, I'll give you the specific words to use when telling your child that someone has died. The Crisis Checklist at the back of this book provides a handy, easy-to-use outline of much of the information I will be presenting here. Turn to it when time is short and you need to know what to say fast.

## DEATH OF A GRANDPARENT

Since the death of a grandparent is often one of the first encounters a child has with death, I'm going to go through this situation in some detail. It is the basic example to build on in other, more specialized, situations.

It's important to get to your child quickly, before friends and other relatives can, so that you can explain in your own way what has happened. Find a quiet place and sit down. Then, talking with the child as calmly and gently as possible, tell him what has happened. First, build the story: say that a very sad thing has happened—that Grandpa has died. If necessary, explain what "dead" means. Next, let him know that you'll be there to help him deal with this; that he's free to talk about how he feels; that he can ask questions and you'll try your best to answer them. I call this making a "communication contract." Finally, describe what will be happening over the next few days and where he fits in—tell him exactly what will happen to him. Children need to hear stories with a beginning, a middle, and an end. Step by step, slowly, give your child the facts in words he or she will easily understand.

Here's what you might say to a five-year-old whose grandfather has died of old age. "A very, very sad thing happened to Grandpa. He was very, very, very old, so old that his body wore out and stopped working. Sometimes when a person is as old as Grandpa was and he gets sick, his body doesn't get better like ours do. It's not strong enough. So it stops working and the person dies because it can't be fixed anymore. That's what happened to Grandpa. That's why everyone is so sad."

Explain that "dead" means the body stopped working and won't do any of the things it used to do. It won't talk, walk, move, see, hear, think. It can't feel anything—it's no longer happy or sad or afraid. It can't feel heat, or cold, or pain. None of the parts of the body work anymore. It can't swallow or go to the bathroom. With a young child you might compare it to the time the goldfish died. (Using flowers or Mr. Hooper from "Sesame Street" as a comparison might be tricky; flowers reappear in the spring and Mr. Hooper comes back in reruns.)

If the person has died from a disease, there are two ways to handle the message to the child, depending on whether the illness was prolonged or sudden. For a prolonged illness, where death has been a process, the child will, I hope, have been informed about the progress of the illness. You might say, "A very sad thing has happened. . . . Usually when people get sick, they get better. But sometimes they get sicker and sicker, and become so weak that their bodies can't fight the sickness anymore, like yours and mine can. And the body wears out and stops working and they die. That's what happened to Grandpa."

Perhaps the illness was a sudden one, like meningitis. "A terrible thing has happened and we are all very sad." (Describe what happened—heart attack, high fever, etc.) "The sickness was so strong and so bad that it wore down his body very fast and he couldn't fight it anymore, so he died. This doesn't happen very often. He didn't know he was going to die and neither did we, so we're surprised and upset."

Tell your child just the basics the first time you sit down together. Tell him only what he needs to know at that moment—that Grandpa is dead, what he died of, and what dead means.

It may be that the child will be stunned, unable to do anything but cry. Right now he's probably not interested in a detailed explanation. Later, he'll have questions, and if you leave the door open, he'll feel free to come and ask them. Human beings seek out only the information they need at a given time.

If possible, tell each child in the family separately, or at least talk to the older ones privately and then the younger ones, making sure that each understands what "dead" means.

Maybe you have great difficulty talking about death. (Maybe it's not just difficult, it's almost impossible for you.) If so, tell your child frankly, "I had a tough time when my grandmother died when I was a kid, and I've never been able to talk about death. But I think it's really important, so I'm going to try it with you." Saying something like this will help put your reaction in perspective for the child—for a moment he or she gets a glimpse of the situation through your eyes. It helps open the lines of communication.

## Avoid Euphemisms

As you're talking with your child, avoid euphemisms. Use words like *dead, stopped working,* and *wore out*—simple words to establish the fact that the body is biologically dead. (Later on, after the child understands that the person is dead forever, you might talk about an afterlife, if this is what you believe.)

*Dead* is a difficult word for some people to say, and many of us go to great lengths to avoid it. When we kill animals, we "put them to sleep." When a person has died, they've "gone away," "passed on," "left us," "checked out." When we adults hear that kind of talk, we can put it in context and decipher the message. We know what the person is saying. A child very often doesn't. Those words don't mean the same thing to a child that they do to an adult. They imply that the dead person willfully abandoned us or that he's trying to find his way back. A child who hears "she lost her father" imagines that maybe he'll be found sometime, maybe he'll come home again. "Gone away" implies a trip, like the time Grandpa went fishing in Vermont. He came back then; maybe he will this time.

Repeating conventional or religious concepts like "He's gone to heaven and he'll live forever" when you're mourning a person who's dead can be very confusing to a youngster. It gives him a mixed message: how can Grandpa be lying in the funeral home, dead, and be up in heaven at the same time? How come Mommy's so upset if Grandpa's going to "live forever"? I'm not suggesting that these concepts be avoided—just that care must be taken to ensure that the child understands the fact of death as well.

One woman I know whose favorite aunt died when she was nine remembers sitting in the church and listening carefully as the minister gave the eulogy describing death as a passing of the seasons. Through the winter, she waited patiently for the spring to come, expecting her aunt to come back with the flowers. She was understandably very upset when the aunt didn't reappear.

Another word to avoid when you're talking with children about death is *sleep*, as one mother I talked with found out.

> "Have you said anything yet to Jennifer about your father?"
>
> "Yes. She knows he's not with us anymore."
>
> "She's four years old now?"
>
> "Right."
>
> "What did you say?"
>
> "Well, when we first came into your office before my father died she wanted to know why he wasn't here, because she expected to see him. I told her he was in the hospital and he was very sick and he wasn't waking up anymore. She asked why we can't wake him up, and I said he's so sick he's

in a very deep sleep, and he may die. And she asked me why and I said, 'because God doesn't want him to be hurting anymore.' And she cried for a while."

I advised that mother to get back to her daughter as quickly as she could and reverse what she had said about sleeping. Her grandfather was definitely not sleeping. When you're sleeping, your eyes are closed but your body still works. When someone is in a coma, his body may not work by itself, and when a person dies, it stops working altogether. Some people who are dead look like they're sleeping, but they're not—they're dead. You don't want the child to think that dead is sleeping, because what happens when Daddy or Jennifer goes to sleep? She'd be afraid that she'd fall asleep, wake up alone, and find that she's buried in the ground.

Another thing to remember when you're talking with children is that God—however you define that term—doesn't kill people. Nor does God go around zapping them because He wants them to be in heaven with Him. Death comes from within the person; the body simply wears out and dies. After you've explained that the person is biologically dead and buried in the cemetery, then you can tell the child about God and an afterlife, if you choose.

## Showing Emotion

Right from the beginning, let your child know that showing emotion is okay. Explain that this is a very, very sad time and that everyone is upset and that many of us may be crying—even Mommy and Daddy. That's because we're sad that we won't see the person anymore because he died. Crying is normal; that's what we feel like doing sometimes when a person dies. You should also explain that many people do *not* show emotion openly when they're upset, but that doesn't mean they didn't love the dead person. If we explain the emotional turmoil that the child feels all around him, he won't be frightened by the change that he sees in us and in others. He'll understand that people may be acting differently than they usually do and he'll see why this is so.

This is an especially important concept to get across to older children. As I've already said, with teenagers you probably won't have to worry about their understanding of death; what they'll need is the facts, and your emotional support and understanding. Without being patronizing, make sure the child understands what you're saying. Remember that he or she may be in shock.

Anna and her husband have two children, aged twelve and thirteen. Their grandfather died of a stroke. He hadn't really been sick, just a little high blood pressure and things of that nature. Then he had a massive stroke. It was a sudden shock for everybody, and there were a lot of feelings bouncing around. I suggested that they say to their children, "Look, if you feel upset about something, talk to us about it."

If you feel upset, too, it's a good idea to talk about it. Many of the parents who've used my program say that sharing their feelings with their children works very well — it helps the children know that what *they're* feeling is okay.

All of this is part of the "communication contract" that you make with your child. Say to the youngster, "Listen, we're not going to hide anything from you. We'll probably all be upset at times and if we feel like crying, that's okay. Sometimes I'll need help. Sometimes we'll talk about Grandpa and the things we remember about him. We're all part of a family and we'll get through this together."

## Explain What Happens Next

After you've gotten across the fact that the person is dead, and you've made your communication contract, the next step is to explain what's going to happen next. What you say will depend, of course, on whether you're religious, and which faith you belong to. For example, here's what I might say to a little one if I were explaining a traditional Christian funeral.

> "Grandpa is going to be moved from the hospital to the funeral home. That's a place where we'll keep Grandpa until the day of the funeral. We have to go to the funeral home soon and speak to the man there about the funeral plans. We'll tell him what clothes we want him to put on Grandpa, and we'll pick out a casket. That's a box we put Grandpa in so that when he gets buried no dirt will get on him [this is important to many children]. Grandpa will be at the funeral home for two days, so that people can come and say prayers and tell everyone how sorry they are. Then we take Grandpa to church, where we'll have a funeral and the priest (minister) will say more prayers. After church we'll go to the cemetery. Grandpa and Grandma picked out a special place there called a grave, and that's where we'll bury Grandpa. Then we put a stone on top of the grave with his name on it. It's a place we can visit and put down some flowers and say a prayer."

For a Jewish service, I would say this:

> "Grandpa is being taken to the funeral home, where we will be able to be with him tomorrow. He will be dressed all in white, and will wear the talis we gave him. He will be in

a casket made of wood. Our family and friends will come to be with us. The rabbi will speak about Grandpa and will pray for him. We will take Grandpa to the cemetery, where he will be placed in the ground. Later on, we'll go back for a visit, and you will be able to place a small stone there as a remembrance of Grandpa. After we return from the cemetery, our relatives and friends will come to visit with us and sit shiva. Daddy and Grandma will both be sitting on boxes [if that is the case]. We will have a candle burning for Grandpa, to remind us how much we loved him and how much we will miss him."

As time goes on, some children will require more explanation, depending on how affected they are by the death. Once the dialogue with your child has been started, though, it should not be too difficult to pick it up again.

Outlining the next few days—where you'll be, where they'll be, and what you'll all be doing—will save them a lot of anxiety. If they can't be with you, knowing what you'll be doing and when you'll be back will ease their minds. The integrity of the family has been shaken and they probably feel insecure. Children like to know where things stand, what to expect, who will take care of them, and where they fit in, and they have a right to know these things.

To a very young one, say something like: "I'm going to the funeral home now and I'll be back at two." Then, pointing to the clock, "That's when the little hand of the clock is right here. Aunt Dot will fix lunch for you and she'll take you to the playground. . . ." And so on, making sure that there are no surprises for the child. Blocking out the time for them will give them a framework to help them adjust in this time of upheaval.

## Questions to Expect

Once you've given your child the information, and gently made sure that he or she has understood what you've said, you can anticipate a variety of questions, which can come right away or several days later. There are several different kinds of questions, and they may be asked directly or indirectly.

*When is he coming back?* First, with the very young child, you'll be asked questions relating to the functioning of the body. The little one who doesn't want to believe that death is final is hoping that at some point you'll give him a "yes" answer, which would mean the body is working again.

Is Grandpa cold in the ground? Is he lonesome, hungry, afraid? When will he be coming home? Hasn't he been dead long enough? Your answer to all these questions is that, "No, he's not lonesome, hungry, cold, etc., because in order to be those things the body has to be working. And Grandpa's body isn't working anymore. He's dead and he won't be coming home anymore . . . ever." Remember to tell your child that this is not like what he sees on TV. The cartoons he watches are make-believe; this is real. Grandpa won't be getting up again. That's why we're so sad; he's dead forever.

"Forever" is a tough concept for anyone to comprehend, but for a child it's really difficult. Tell him you're going to take him to the movies on Friday and he'll say, "Friday! That's such a long time!" His time is marked by the mileposts in his life—Christmas, his birthday, when he starts school. From September to December can seem like an eternity. He just doesn't understand "forever."

*How old are you?* This is another of the basic questions that will turn up in different forms. One father at first didn't buy the ideas I've been outlining here; he told me that his six-year-old was taking it all very well, that he understood what "dead" means and that he wasn't in the least bit concerned about his grandmother's death. A couple of days after the funeral the child spent quite a bit of time with a pencil and paper, writing down and adding up numbers. Later, while his mother was giving him a bath, he made a remark that caused his father to reverse his position about talking to children about death. "I've been doing some adding and I've figured out how old you are, Mommy," the child proclaimed. "And Daddy, too! You're seventy-three and he's eighty-seven." That child certainly calculated wrong—his father was in his early 30's! But behind that child's observation was the fear of his parents' death. Remember, age and death are connected in a child's mind. He has little understanding of the degrees of time or age, or how old is *old*. In the mind of a little one, babies are "newer," a teenager is older, and everyone over twenty, including his parents, is really long in the tooth. What you have to do is make him understand that Grandpa was so old he was two times as old as Daddy and Mommy.

Here's an answer to the "Are you going to die, too?" questions related to the question of age: "Everyone dies sometime. But I don't expect to die until you are very old and have children of your own. Once in a while people get very sick or get in a very bad accident; then they die before they're very, very old. But most of the time people don't die until they're very, very, *very* old."

*"Why did he have to die? Why couldn't he get better?"* The third basic question that your youngsters may ask has to do with why the person died, and why he couldn't be cured. It's not enough to say, "Grandpa got a pain in his stomach and died." A child's mind might handle that information this

way: "I had a tummy ache last week and I felt sick. Maybe I'm going to die now." Because he draws from his own experience, a child's knowledge is limited. So you have to work to get across how sick Grandpa really was . . . so sick that the child has never experienced anything like it. As we've seen, a young child takes things literally and connects things that don't belong together. He may hear someone say, "Boy, that flu really got to me. I was so sick I could have died!" Assure the youngster that Grandpa's sickness was different from the times each of you get sick. "Grandpa was very, very, very sick. Not sick like you feel when you get a tummy ache. Not sick like Daddy gets when he gets a headache. Not sick like Mommy when she gets a cough." There was something wrong with the way Grandpa's body was working. Explain that your bodies are normal, and that when you get sick your bodies are strong enough to fight the sickness and make it go away. Grandpa's body couldn't do that. Some things can't be fixed. So he died.

*"Did I do it?"* A final question children often ask has to do with responsibility. Couldn't somebody have saved him? Couldn't it have been someone else? Explain that sometimes bad things happen in this world. Since everyone in the world has to die sometime, the people who love them are going to be sad and miss them just like we miss Grandpa. There's nothing anyone could have done. No one caused Grandpa to die (unless there were special circumstances, which we'll discuss later on). Add that sometimes children feel that they said or did something that caused Grandpa to die, but that's just not so. People die because their bodies stopped working.

The "I did it" syndrome, or misdirected thinking, isn't confined just to the minds of children. How often we adults blame ourselves for the death of a loved one! "If only I had gotten him to the hospital on time." "If only I had tried harder to get him to stop smoking." As children get older, they often have these reactions, common to grieving adults. The clue to their thinking might be questions like, "Couldn't the doctors have given him just one more blood transfusion?" or a statement such as, "If only I had called the ambulance faster." What the child may really be asking is, "Am I in any way responsible for this? Is there any way I could have prevented it?" Your answer to him or her is "No." Taking a logical look at the facts, you explain that there's nothing he or she could have done.

As children get older, many of their questions will have to do with changing relationships. Who will take care of Grandma now that Grandpa is dead? How is this going to affect our family? What about me? Who's going to read me stories now that he is dead? Underneath these questions are feelings of insecurity and unrest. By giving your child the facts, letting him know what to expect, and making him a part of the group, you'll ease a lot of those fears.

Over the days and weeks following a death, children may ask these questions again and again in slightly different ways. If they ask something that you can't answer, be honest and say you don't know. It's better to admit that you don't understand something than to fill a child's mind with a deception or half-truth. Tell him that death is a tough subject, a mystery, and that you don't know everything. But don't let that be a cop-out, either. Children deserve answers to their questions, given on a level that they'll understand. If you can't explain something, find someone who can. If you're very disturbed at the time your child asks a question, hug him or her and say, "I can't talk about it now, I'm too upset. We'll talk about it later." But follow through on your promise, so the child doesn't feel put off.

Trying to cover every eventuality, making sure that every question is anticipated, is, of course, an impossible task. What we aim for is to be sensitive and open to our children. As you listen to their questions, you'll find out more about what they are thinking. One mother told her four-year-old only that Grandpa had died and gone to heaven. As they walked in the door of the funeral home, the mother was stopped in her tracks by the child's question, "Is this heaven?" The mother knew she'd have to backtrack and explain what was what. "I realized at that point that what I had been saying to her was not correct."

## The Question of an Afterlife

Each family has to handle the question of an afterlife in its own way, and sometimes the views of your friends and relatives will differ from your own. Try to get across what you believe as quickly as possible, so that your child will have a firm foundation before others have their say.

Sometimes well-meaning relatives, sharing their religious beliefs in an attempt to comfort the child, can cause a great deal of confusion. Take the statement, "God loved Grandpa, and He took him to heaven." What seems like a valid, if simply stated, religious belief can give the child a very different message: "God loves Mommy and Daddy and me, too. Maybe we'll all be taken away like Grandpa."

I am in no way discounting the importance of religious conviction, but faith involves believing what you cannot see, trusting, and being willing to wait for the answer, and it's a tough thing for many children. It's a wonderful gift, and people who have faith often are much better able to deal with their grief and feelings of loss than those who don't. Children who have been prepared with a good biological explanation of why the person died may then be ready for the explanation of what happens after life. Religion can be a beautiful ending to the story of what happened to Grandpa. But problems occur when people use it as a beginning, middle, and end to the story, without saying anything else.

## DEATH OF AN IMMEDIATE FAMILY MEMBER (MOTHER, FATHER, SIBLING)

According to a report issued in 1984 by the National Academy of Sciences, the children most deeply affected by a death in their immediate family are usually young children who have lost their mothers, or teenagers whose fathers have died. But any child who has had death hit so close to home usually has a very difficult time.

Dolores Callahan, describing her family's experience in an article in *Thanatos*, a journal on bereavement, pointed out that in a family we interact by drawing from and contributing to each other's lives. When her sister died, "all of a sudden a piece of the pie was missing." Not only did the family lose the sister and her unique personality, but the family design was ripped apart, its wholeness shattered, and because of that each of the members felt diminished. "It's hard to accept. We felt disfigured by her loss."

Children are not supposed to die. They're expected to live long, productive lives. So when a child dies, the parents sometimes feel so disturbed and helpless that for a while they can't maintain a healthy relationship with their other children or with each other. Three-quarters of the couples who experience the death of a child separate or divorce. The family is thrown into turmoil. Parents sometimes expect one of the other siblings to take the place of the dead child, and sometimes they retreat into themselves, shutting out the other children. That can be very harmful to a child, who learns how to grieve by watching his or her parents.

"What was it like for my parents when Gene died?" asks Claudia Typond in *The Death of a Child—A Case Study.* "They surely went through some kind of hell, yet I never saw it. All that was visible was a wall of silence."

A child picks up on the anxiety that his parents are feeling, and it often feeds on his own fears. The sidekick he lived with and played with and fought with and laughed with is dead. Her bike is still in the garage. Her rock albums are still next to the stereo. She was part of the family's life, and yet she's not here anymore. "If it happened to my own sister, it can happen to me," he may be thinking. "Will it happen tomorrow or next week?". . . "Mommy doesn't love me anymore. She's always crying even though it's been such a long time since Jimmy died. She probably wishes I had died instead." Young children may also lose some of their confidence in their parents' ability to protect them from harm.

These are some of the thoughts that may be milling around in the child's mind, and his behavior may well reflect his distress. Matthew wanted to make everything right in the family again. Although not a very athletic fellow, he took up football, trying to fill the slot his brother, "the jock," had left. Confused and angry, six-year-old Steven refused to do his schoolwork, sitting passively in the corner while the rest of the class worked around him. He just didn't know what to say.

The situation can be even worse for a child when the parent dies. Irwin was a teenager, very busy juggling school and work, but nearly every bit of extra time he had was spent at the hospital, next to the bedside of his sick father. One evening Irwin took a break, went out for dinner with a friend, then went racing back to the hospital room to spend the rest of the evening with his dad. "My father was gone. The mattress was rolled up on the bed," Irwin says. "I'll never forget that scene. I never got a chance to tell him good-bye." And yet, if you had met Irwin that evening, you would never have known he was that deeply upset.

Children grieve differently from adults. Instead of experiencing intense distress, many children are likely at first to deny the death, then grieve intermittently for many years. Experts point out that because of this, they can suffer emotional disturbances that carry over into adulthood.

In her book *How It Feels When a Parent Dies*, Jill Krementz talked with eight youngsters ranging in age from seven to sixteen. One child whose grief was more immediately apparent told her, "When Mom told me that Daddy was dead, my knees started shaking. I almost fell down. My sister Peg screamed when she found out. My hands still shake when I think about my father." Another was plagued with nightmares. "I had a dream that she was lying at the bottom of a closet and she came back to life. When I have dreams like that, I just pinch myself on the arm to see if I'm awake or dreaming."

Nightmares are not uncommon when a close family member dies. Since it's awfully hard to break the spiritual connection with someone who has been so close to you, other family members may hear the dead person laugh or cry, or may imagine that he appears to them in a mystical experience. Paul Patterson of the Albany Medical College said that these experiences are often strikingly similar to the grief-induced hallucinations that occur during the transfer from sleep to awakening in the morning. Just as people are coming out of their dreams, "when our unconscious is most

susceptible to control . . . our minds produce the phenome-
non of the spirit hovering over the body."

What do you say to children when someone so close to
them dies unexpectedly? When a brother or sister they grew
up with, or a parent they idolized, is suddenly dead, and the
family seems to be shattered? Perhaps you might explain it
to a child around the age of five in this way. (Of course,
you'll also want to add some of the basic information, such
as what "dead" means, which we discussed in the section on
the death of a grandparent.)

> "Sometimes terrible things happen to us in life, and
> something terrible has happened to our family. Your brother
> Jimmy has died. He got very, very, very sick with a disease
> not many people get, and he died very fast. It's nobody's
> fault because no one could have saved him. There are some
> things we just can't understand. We'll miss Jimmy awfully
> because we won't be seeing him again, and we loved him,
> and he loved us very much. But even without Jimmy we'll
> still always be a family, and we'll stick together."

If you have older children, you'll have to tailor the
explanation to fit their needs. As I pointed out in the last
chapter, preteens will probably be interested in the techni-
cal details of how the death occurred, for example, while a
nine-year-old would need to be reassured that death is not
contagious. Above all, don't adhere rigidly to my suggestions for the level of information needed by different age
groups. You know your children better than anyone else
does, so use this material only as a guide.

When one parent dies, another issue that almost always
comes up is concern about the other parent. "What will

happen to me if you also die?" the child wonders. Be prepared to answer this question honestly and reassuringly.

The way in which children work through their grief depends a lot on how their parents and the other members of their family handle themselves, and whether or not the other family members reach out to them. The stronger the state of the helping adult, the better off the child will be. If the adult encourages the child to grieve, lets him know how much the dead person loved him and what joy the child brought to him, the youngster will be better able to cope. Also, if life is kept relatively stable, it will make things a lot easier for the child.

This sense of stability is not an easy thing for parents to maintain. Since a death in the immediate family is such a blow, some parents are not able to cope with the death themselves, much less help their kids. Elise Longpré, whose husband died in a car crash, advises grieving families not to be afraid to go for help, She contacted Mothers Against Drunk Drivers (MADD), a victim support group. "I had been independent till now and it never crossed my mind to accept any help," she wrote in *Thanatos*. "In fact, I would refuse when someone offered their help." But she decided that she had to change. "I found myself accepting help and each time it became easier. Because of this, I am mingling more with people now." There are a number of other support groups, such as Compassionate Friends, that help families in crisis; I've listed some of them in the back of this book. Very often, however, a family will need the help of a trained professional to make it through the grief.

A few final suggestions on dealing with the death of a family member:

First, let the children know who would take care of them

if you died, and to whom they should go for help in an emergency. They think about such things; they'll feel more secure if they know what to expect.

Second, let the family share in the ritual of grieving. If a child's brother has died, for example, let him put his brother's special toys in the casket beside him. Older children can be pallbearers; younger ones can put flowers on the altar.

Finally, as the family grieves, help each member find some kind of identification with the dead person. One young boy constantly wore his dead brother's high-school letter jacket, even though it swallowed him up. A fourteen-year-old girl helped her father finish stripping a table the mother had been working on. In the next chapter, I'll talk about the processes of grief and healing in more detail.

Can anything good come out of the death of someone we love? At first you think, absolutely not. But sometimes when we are confronted with loss, grieving can help us find more direction in our lives. As people suffer they often become more open to others, and in the crisis start sharing their feelings and thoughts with other members of their family, perhaps after years of keeping things to themselves. A crisis sometimes brings out the best in people. "After this, I know I can handle anything," one mother said. "I know now that our family will stick together and who our friends are. What living is is having other people. When Joe died, it was those other people who helped us get through. Lovely, lovely people. Thank God we had our friends."

## If a Member of Your Family Is Dying

Very often when I sit down with a family to make funeral arrangements, I begin by asking if the children knew this person was sick. The parents will often say yes, they knew he was sick, but they didn't know that he was dying. Then, when the person dies, the children are very often shocked. "She might just as well have been hit by a bus," one young man remarked. "We had no idea she was going to die."

When a loved one is dying, the others in the family experience "anticipatory grief," according to Dr. Paul Patterson. Even before the death occurs, since they know it's coming, the adults already begin to mourn for the person. Children pick up on that grief. Dr. Patterson advises parents to be honest with their children about the dying person's chances of survival. If the odds are only ten percent, say so.

During the final months and days before a death, the demands on the parents are enormous. Overwhelmed with their own feelings of grief, they sometimes withdraw from their children; this can be highly upsetting to the youngsters, who are anxious about being abandoned. When the family does stay united in its attempt to cope with grief— when all the family members understand what was going on, and the children are involved and can help out a bit— everyone benefits from the experience.

## INFANT DEATH

When a newborn baby dies, it's the closest thing to insanity most parents could ever imagine. I know—my first-born son, Daniel, died when he was not yet a day old.

In those days, twenty years ago, when a baby was born dead or died shortly after birth, it was thought that the best thing to do was to quickly bury the child with no wake or funeral, so Daniel was taken directly to the cemetery. My wife, Barbara, never saw her first son. Although she very much wanted to see him, I wouldn't let her. There was no question in my mind that I was doing the right thing. I had talked to our relatives about what you do in a situation like this and they explained the way it was handled. The hospital people, the priest, the family—everyone agreed that I should spare her the pain of seeing her dead child. "Get it over with so she'll forget about it," they said.

I went along with what other people said, against the wishes of my wife, doing what I felt was right, what I thought was best for her. It wasn't until some years later, when Barbara and I began discussing our feelings about Daniel, that I saw how I had been trying to make believe the child had never existed. I had so thoroughly pushed the experience out of my mind that when I was first working on this chapter, I couldn't even remember what month the baby had been born.

Barbara wasn't able to block out Daniel as effectively as I was. When a baby dies, a parent—especially the mother—never forgets, never really stops the grieving. Sure, the pain lessens over time, but it's impossible to eradicate it. Tina Russo Quirk, a nurse writing about infant death in the *Journal of Nurse-Midwifery*, called it "one of the loneliest of losses," with no wake, no flowers, no memories to share.

Another complication that aggravates the grieving process is one involving self-image. Often, when a newborn dies the parents feel that they were somehow responsible, that something must have been wrong with them physically, causing them to produce a defective child. This feeling of guilt can be especially strong if Sudden Infant Death Syndrome is the cause of the baby's death (we'll discuss this in more detail shortly). Absorbed in their grief and shame, parents sometimes blame each other, the doctors, and God. These desperate feelings are naturally picked up by the other children in the family.

## Relating to and Helping the Other Children

In an article published in *Pediatrics* magazine, Barbara Elliott, a nurse whose twin sons died when they were just a
week old, talked about how tough it was for her and her husband to relate to their other children, ages two and four.
"The two-year-old kept repeating, 'Babies out of tummy, babies dead. No more babies.' The four-year-old understood
our sadness and knew the babies were never coming home."
Mrs. Elliott said that after a series of bad days at home, the
four-year-old returned to preschool and that seemed to help.
But she still had a hard time caring for her youngsters. "I
was so wrapped up in my own feelings that I could not see
how much they needed me. I was intolerant of them. Then
the two-year-old got the flu. As his fever rose, I kept thinking
what it would be like if he died, too. Then I knew how
much he needs me, and how much I needed him to love. I
was jolted. I knew I had not been able to support or find joy
in them."

"I've lost my ability to love. I just can't give anymore."
That's how many parents whose newborns have died feel for
a while. It's hard to be patient with little children who are
picking up the vibrations in the family that all is not well,
and are acting up because of it.

Trying to help the other children come to terms with
what has happened is the most difficult part of coping with
the death. Cleveland psychologist Edna Furman, who has
been working with bereaved children for 30 years, says,
"Why is it so difficult? In part, it is because the feelings of
the children about the newborn baby are so totally different
from the parent's feelings. . . . To the children, and to young
children in particular, this baby was not looked forward to as
a cherished newcomer—it was a potential rival without

whom they could have easily gotten along happily in life." Furman adds that the questions the child is likely to ask—"Can it happen to me and to you, Mommy?" or "Was it your fault, Mommy, or was it my fault?"—are especially difficult for the parent to answer.

To explain to the children why a baby has been born dead or has lived for just a few hours, a parent can say the following: "Sometimes when a new baby is born, it's very, very sick, so sick that his body stops working and dies." Explain the cause of death, if you know it (that his lungs were not developed, for example). "It's nothing that anybody did or forgot to do. Doctors are not sure why it happens, but with our little baby, his body didn't grow correctly and all of his parts inside were not working right, so he died."

St. John's Hospital in Springfield, Illinois, offers a list of suggestions for helping families who have lost a newborn child:

- Name the child. This helps to include the baby in the family's life and helps recognize the child's existence.
- Keep a memory book, a tangible record of the family's feelings during the time of loss.
- Have a picture taken of the baby and dispose of the baby's things yourselves. That acknowledges that the baby lived and died.
- A birth certificate with footprints should be made up. Both parents should be involved in the decision of whether or not there should be an autopsy, and both parents should also decide on the burial plans. These joint decisions help promote family communication.

- Each parent should decide if he or she wants to hold the dead baby.

Most parents I've talked to said they benefited from seeing their dead baby. Even in cases where the child was born badly deformed, parents have tended to look at the normal parts of the child, saying things like, "Well, all his toes are there and his fingers are fine." Seeing the baby often helps parents to better accept the death.

Should a dead child's brothers and sisters be allowed to attend the funeral? Furman suggests that adolescents should be allowed to decide for themselves; younger children, if they are accompanied by their parents, are also usually helped by attending the funeral. Most experts agree that it's really up to the individual family.

## Sudden Infant Death Syndrome

One of the most traumatic things that can happen to a family is to have a baby die from Sudden Infant Death Syndrome (SIDS). Apparently healthy one minute, then dead the next, the child suddenly stops breathing. Unexpected and so far unexplained, SIDS is the cause of an estimated 7,000 deaths annually,[1] usually in the children's first year. Families are left in a state of shock, having to cope with denial, anger, and depression.

Today, with the new public awareness of child abuse, the parent whose child has been a victim of SIDS often ends up defensively explaining that the death was not caused by any-

---

[1]According to Christine Blenninger, project coordinator for the New York City Information and Counseling Program for Sudden Infant Death.

thing he did or did not do. For many, it's not a sufficient explanation. "What do you mean, you don't know what the baby died of?" In this age when medical science has answers for everything, the fact that there's no answer for SIDS is incomprehensible to some people. If the baby died of some disease that people had heard of, there'd be no further need to explain, no need for more questions. But most of the time with SIDS, they don't understand.

Because of the senselessness of SIDS, because the parents have such a hard time coming to grips with it, this type of death is especially hard to explain to the other children in the family. Here are a few words, necessarily very simple, that you can say to a little child whose brother or sister has died from SIDS.

> "Sometimes with little babies something happens that makes their bodies stop working. It's hard to explain because no one's sure what it is, but that's what happens sometimes. It's nothing anyone did or forgot to do. It just happened."

Older children who need more of an explanation should be told what was *not* the cause of SIDS. Here's what the National SIDS Clearinghouse tells us: A SIDS death was not anyone's fault; not hereditary or contagious; not caused by external suffocation, by vomiting, or by choking. SIDS infants do not suffer when they die. It could not have been predicted or prevented by anyone. A medical reality that can be determined only by an autopsy, SIDS can strike any family, suddenly and silently, usually during periods of sleep.

Emphasize to the children that SIDS kills infants, not older children, so they won't be afraid that they will die when they go to sleep. Finally, let the child know that it's happened to many other babies as well—it's the major cause of death in the period after the first month until the end of the first year.

The Children's Hospital in Boston conducted a study on the effect of a SIDS death on the other siblings in the family. Researchers found that the trauma greatly affected the children. Eighty percent of the children studied showed changes in their behavior patterns. Because of SIDS, the family structure was abruptly altered. Big brother and big sister roles were suddenly terminated in a catastrophic manner, and the children were knocked off-balance for a while. Some of the youngsters regressed in their toilet training and some had trouble eating; others had problems interacting with their playmates, and most had trouble sleeping. Unable to understand what had happened to their apparently healthy brother or sister, they were confused, disrupted, and afraid of going to bed at night. In the Boston study, one three-year-old described her nightmare: a monster was coming to take her because she had killed her baby brother. A second child dreamed that a monster was coming to take her to heaven to be with her brother. Another child had night terrors, frightening episodes where in the middle of the night the youngster started screaming. Her mother understood: "She was right here when it happened [when the baby died], and I was screaming. She wakes up screaming now. I have to lie down with her to get her to go back to sleep."

Some of the SIDS parents in the study, not knowing which way to turn, spoiled their other children in their need to be close to them. "Holding him brought me comfort that no one else could. I had to know that he was safe and I could only know that by holding onto him." Others distanced themselves from their children for a while. "I couldn't stand to be near her. I was afraid of what would happen."

Sometimes the confused children lashed out, but sometimes they reassured their parents. "It's okay," said one little child, talking about his dead brother. "He's in heaven with the angels." Another told her mother, "Don't be too sad, you still have me." One mother said that she didn't know who needed more hugging, her child or herself.

Hugging—sometimes that's about all you can do after you've told your child that this baby brother or sister has died. Hugging, and answering questions, and crying together. It will be a long time before your family will be able to make sense out of this . . . if you ever do. For a long time you'll be struggling with the feelings of guilt and grief and the question, "What happened?"

How this death is dealt with will have a lasting effect on your other children. It's probably the first time they've ever experienced a death, especially one so close to them, someone dear whom they watched grow bigger and helped take care of. Let your children share your grief. Accept their feelings, taking care not to work out your own grief through them.

When friends come to visit and offer their condolences, don't send your young one out of the room. He may think something terrible will happen again or that everyone is talking about him. He feels very insecure right now. He needs your support and your love . . . and to know you won't leave him. Open discussions, where he'll get the answers he needs, are a must for a family victimized by the death of an infant. By talking out their feelings, by helping them draw pictures or write down what's on their minds, they'll express how they feel and work out the grief.

Most parents and professionals I've talked to said that once a child is old enough to understand what is going on, taking him to the funeral is a good idea. The ritual gives him a framework in which to start the grieving process. (For more about involving children in the funeral, see Chapter 5.)

## DEATH OF A FRIEND OR CLASSMATE

When a child's friend or classmate dies, it can be almost as shattering to a youngster as if a close family member had died. That's because the teachers and classmates make up a kind of second family for the child. It is at school that children spend most of their day and much of their free time, so it's natural for the child to be very upset if someone at school dies.

Francis De Bernardo, writing in *The Tablet*, a Catholic newspaper in New York City, interviewed children who had watched their high school teacher collapse and die during chemistry class at Bishop Ford High School in Brooklyn. "One moment he was standing there and then he grabbed his chest . . . and fell to the floor," one child remembered. The students went into action, some of them aiding the dying teacher, others ushering their classmates, gasping and crying, out of the classroom.

For many of those teenagers, this was their first direct experience with death, and several months later when De Bernardo talked with them they were still trying hard to accept it. Among the questions they asked themselves was, "Why did it have to be our classroom?" Father Jim Devlin, assistant chaplain at the school, explained to them that it is very normal to feel angry because death is often so irrational. "There are some things that can't be explained away." Since their teacher's death was so sudden and hard to comprehend, many of the youngsters felt guilty, thinking that somehow they could have saved him. Others pushed it out of their minds. One boy said he tried to talk to his mother but he couldn't say anything. Another said he'd learned to appreciate people more, not to take them so much for granted. Suddenly aware of how quickly death can come, one child realized that life is a precious gift—and so are his parents. "I realized that . . . there's no age limit. I thought I should show them I love them more . . . get closer to them."

*The Compassionate Friends Newsletter* suggests that since the class functions as a group, the students might share grief as a class. The teacher might read a library book on death and grieving with the class; lead a classroom discussion; make a scrapbook; or plant a memorial tree. But most of all, say the Compassionate Friends, the teacher can be there to talk with.

One of the positive by-products of the tragic increase in teenage suicides in recent years has been the establishment of courses in death and dying in a number of high schools. In these courses, adolescents learn why some people choose to kill themselves, what the danger signals are for suicide, and how they can go to their teacher or another adult for help if they hear any of their friends talking about suicide, or are contemplating it themselves. Openness in talking about suicide, and about death in general, removes much of the mystique that can make it appealing to youngsters; it also helps break the chain reaction that can develop after one suicide occurs in a community.

The benefits of grieving together can extend to a whole community. In July 1979, six teenagers on their way to work in the cornfields near Sandwich, Illinois, were killed in a car crash. "Six of Sandwich's finest—its cheerleaders, the prom queen, track stars, choir girls—were dead. Instantly, with no preparation. No chance to say good-bye," wrote Barbara Snyder in the *Buffalo News* (N.Y.). Dr. Carol Troescher, a grief counselor originally from Buffalo, New York, was working in a town near Sandwich. She immediately contacted the Sandwich School Superintendent, asked what she could do to help, and ended up working in Sandwich for two years. As Dr. Troescher put it, the town was like a mosaic with six of its bright, colorful stones missing; she had to keep the mosaic from "becoming unglued."

She sat around kitchen tables and looked at photo albums as the families talked about the girls they lost. "There's Paula on the track team. . . . She was stubborn . . . had a great sense of humor." They needed to reminisce about their loss. Sometimes the kids had to remind their parents not to focus all their attention on their dead sisters. Finally, as the months and years passed—after they had said, "That's enough"—the people of Sandwich began to heal. Dr. Troescher explained, "They realized there was nothing they could do. They asked, 'What is this going to do to our lives? Is this going to kill us? Is this going to break us apart? Or are we going to go on living?' " Some families were torn apart; other families pulled together.

Dr. Troescher conducted classes on dealing with grief at the high school; she brought in speakers and invited the students to share their poetry and music that helped them through the calamity. But, reports Snyder, the most dramatic and tangible thing that came out of the tragedy at Sandwich was a booklet called "Thanks for the Memories," a collection of poems, stories, and sketches about the dead girls, done by their friends and families . . . the reminiscenses of a community that mourned, then pulled out of grief.

## ACCIDENTAL DEATH

"Life," say Audrey Gordon and Dennis Klaus in *They Need to Know*, "at times may be something to cry about." When death is a result of old age, or is a slow, gradual passing away, the family is given a little time to prepare for the inevitable. In the case of an accident, death comes as a terrific shock. The family feels victimized; something or someone has taken control of fate. A mother, talking with her friends in the park, looks away for a moment and her child runs into the street and is hit by a car.

When there's an accident, the family is often laden with anger and guilt. Mothers Against Drunk Drivers (MADD) have a right to be angry at those who drink and drive, and they're channeling their anger, making it quite productive. Undoubtedly lives will be saved by their efforts. But the guilt experienced by the child who accidentally broke his brother's neck while they were rough-housing is hard to channel. He feels responsible. That child may live for a lifetime with guilt unless he gets some professional help. People need to learn that sometimes bad things just happen, as Harold Kushner points out in his book *When Bad Things Happen to Good People*, and there's nothing anyone can do about it.

Children are usually able to comprehend death from an accident more easily than just about any other kind of death, because parents are always making such a big deal about how they should avoid them. "Don't go near the window. You might fall out." "Watch when you're crossing the street so you don't get hit by a car."

And so, when you're explaining a death caused by an accident, relate it back to something they've heard before: "You know how Mommy and Daddy are always telling you to be careful when you're crossing the street, because there are crazy drivers who could hit you? Well, a terrible thing has happened to Uncle Bill. . . ." Explain what happened in the accident. Go through the basic information about everybody being sad that the person is dead. Then explain why: "His body was hurt so badly that it couldn't be fixed, so it stopped working and he's dead."

## MURDER

The headlines read, "Hero Cop Slain by Freak Shot in Siege." It was a warm September day and Susan was on her way out the door of her house, looking for her older son to take him for a haircut. "And all of a sudden, my neighbor drives up. He's with the town police. I could see from his face that something was wrong. 'Something's happened,' I said. 'Tell me right now, I know it's bad.' 'Joe's been shot,' the neighbor said. 'He didn't make it.' "

Susan didn't faint, she didn't go into hysterics. "Let me think for a moment," she said. "Please find my children." Within moments, fifteen policemen helicoptered into the little village, landed in the schoolyard nearby, then descended on her house. Without a word, they pushed past her through the door and combed the house. "My God, what's happening?" she said. Later, she was told that they were looking for a gun, afraid that Susan, in her grief, might kill herself.

What kind of effect will a scene like that have on the children in the family? In his work at New York's Harlem Hospital Center, Dr. Hal Fishkin has dealt with a number of youngsters whose parents have been murdered. "It's going to have a permanent impact on the child's life. Some children are resilient and can deal with it, but others, the vulnerable ones, need a particular sensitivity." Fishkin says that it's tough in a time of crisis for policemen, neighbors, and emergency room personnel to think about the children and about what's happening inside their minds—but it's necessary.

Fortunately, most children won't have to face what Susan's family did—the murder of someone close to them. But when it does happen, the child often experiences serious problems that may require professional help.

In an article in *Monitor*, a publication for psychologists, Carol Turkington quoted Alvin Pouissant of the Harvard Medical School, who studied the reactions of children victimized by murder. "They felt violated—like rape victims— they wanted to seek revenge and hunt for the killer, and they exhibited terror of their environment."

Each child reacts differently. Jan lay in bed with a pair of pinking shears clutched in her hand for protection. Betsy couldn't go back into her house until the walls had been painted a different color, so the place wouldn't seem the same. Timothy, who watched as his mother was shot, dreams about killing the murderer.

Child psychologist Dr. Robert Pynoos of UCLA says that a child who's suffered through such a trauma will "hear that gunshot forever." Not only does the child have a horrible image to contend with, he is also plagued with the urge to pay the murderer back, so he imagines ways he'd execute him. This is especially traumatic if one parent killed the other. "The ambivalent urges to revenge the slain parent and to protect the remaining parent can never be satisfactorily resolved without some form of psychiatric treatment. . . . To see your parent killed is an event a child never recovers from."

What do you say to a child after someone he or she loves has been murdered? Begin by stating something along these lines: "Sometimes things happen in life—terrible things that we have no control over. Well, a terrible thing has happened." Explain that the person was murdered—shot or stabbed or whatever—and tell the child who did it: "A bad man we don't know . . ." "Uncle John went crazy and shot Daddy. . . ."

Explain as simply as possible what happened, who did it, and why—if you know. Then try to help your child deal with the trauma. It's going to be tough if the person was a key figure in his social structure. If it was his mother or father, the death will have a profound effect on him, regardless of whether or not he was close to that parent or perhaps even hated him or her. His whole social system has been upset, and, as the late Harvard psychiatrist Erich Lindeman noted, the child needs to break the strong ties that he had to the dead person, to find other people to get close to.

When you're dealing with a murder, it's particularly important to involve the child in the funeral and the family's mourning process, to help the child stay in touch with reality. Also, as a way of softening the trauma, many experts suggest letting the child relive the experience, perhaps encouraging him or her to draw the scene of the murder in detail. Dr. Hal Fishkin says that when he's working with youngsters who have witnessed a death, whether it's a murder or an accident, he gets the child to relate all the details so he can find out what the child thinks happened. He compares these perceptions to what the police or other sources say actually happened. "You try to reconcile the two stories so you can know what the child is thinking," Fishkin advises. If the child describing the murder says, "He got mad at me and beat me," then the child may think it was his fault that the person got angry and killed his mother. "I might say something like, 'Well, your mother had terribly bad luck when she met him, because he's not a good man.' And you try to deal with the guilt and anger."

Eventually, as the months pass, new feelings will come out of the child. After six months, says Fishkin, the child will not be as enraged or depressed. "The big question is, do you allow the child to cover over and forget about it, or do you bring it up? That's a very hard thing to generalize. Different children need different things. With some, there's a turbulent, emotional response at the time of the trauma and you want to help them cover over . . . give them some support for their defenses. But with others—they're withdrawn and you know that there's a kind of precancerous growth inside that you have to excise in some way. You have to bring it out." In any case, therapy is almost always necessary to help the child deal with depression, desire for revenge, and loss of faith in the order of society.

## SUICIDE

One of the most difficult kinds of death that a family ever has to cope with is one in which one family member feels directly responsible for the death of another. This is often the case with suicide. Prompted by hopelessness, despondency, or anxiety, the person who kills himself makes a statement to the world that he can't bear to live anymore. The survivors often feel that he willfully abandoned them— that he didn't want to be around them anymore, that he didn't care what would happen. For those who are left behind, it's the ultimate rejection.

Experts say that suicide is almost always the expression of

a malfunction in the family system—an attempt to manipulate relationships in an inflexible family structure, or the revenge of a person who feels that no one cares and that he can no longer cope. UCLA researcher Dr. Edwin Shneidman says, "Psychodynamically, suicide can be seen as murder turned 180 degrees."

Because of this, suicide leaves the family members permanently changed. It's an act that breeds turmoil and self-doubt as the bereaved try to comprehend it, all the while punishing themselves with recriminations. Because of the stigma attached to suicide, some people attempt to run away from the reality of it, making the situation even worse for any children in the family.

John Brogan and Ula Maiden teach a death and dying course to seventh- and eighth-graders in Yorktown Heights, New York. Several years ago, they noticed that one of their students, Trudy, was very obviously depressed. One day, Trudy ran into their classroom, agitated; she pushed by Ula, gave her pocketbook to a friend, then went running down the hall. John took off after her, grabbed her, and saw that she had tried to cut her wrists. In her pocketbook were bottles of medicine that she had planned to take and a suicide note addressed to her friend. Hysterical, she was taken to the hospital and admitted to a psychiatric ward.

The students in that class watched the whole scene unfold. On the bus the next day, they naturally were talking about it. Also on the bus was Trudy's twelve- year-old brother, just one year younger than Trudy, who had no idea what everyone was talking about. When he found out that his sister had attempted suicide, he was shocked. Sure, he had noticed that his sister hadn't come home the night before, but his parents hadn't told him why. He had just assumed she was away at a friend's house.

When you're faced with a suicide attempt or an actual suicide, in which all questions of accident have been ruled out and people know what happened, refusing to talk about it with your children or to admit that it happened can be very traumatic for them. One boy came home after school and found his father lying in the living room with a gunshot wound in his head. His mother later told the child that his father had died of a heart attack. The child knew better; he would never forget that horrendous scene. Lying or withholding the truth destroys the child's not-fully-developed trust in those around him, and contributes to the chaotic atmosphere charged with stigma, guilt, anger, and betrayal. It's far better to have a loved one tell him the truth, in a simple but honest way, than to have to hear about it outside the home, where people might not be so kind. It's not a question of whether or not to tell the children, but rather how to tell them, when, and what to say.

Of course, coping with suicide involves more than simply talking out your feelings. In almost all cases, experts agree that the family should have professional help. Because suicide has an impact different from any other kind of death, there are all sorts of psychological complications—such as the fact that suicides sometimes repeat in a family—that should be dealt with by experienced counselors. Before talking with your child about a suicide, it's a good idea to consult a professional. After you have done so, here are some suggestions as to how you can open the lines of communication with your child.

First of all, the experts I've talked to stress that it's important to find out exactly what happened before talking with the child. If you're sure the suicide was intentional—when there is no doubt that the person planned to kill him or herself—you might say: "Sometimes a person's body gets sick and doesn't work right. Sometimes a person's mind doesn't work right. He can't see things clearly and he feels the only way to solve this problem is by ending his life. That's what happened here. . . ."

If you're not sure the death was actually a suicide—if the death was due to something like a drug or alcohol over-dose—you might say, "Sometimes people take pills to relax, or to get to sleep, or to try to block out their problems. These pills make a person's body slow down, but too many make the body stop working. We don't know that he wanted to die, but that's what happened." To an older child you might add more information: "He had a very serious problem and he went through a period of weakness. If he had given himself time, he wouldn't have found it necessary to kill himself. This was the worst solution he could have chosen. But we have to try to understand him; he wasn't thinking clearly when he did it. You might be feeling angry with him—that it's unfair to you for him to have chosen this solution. That's okay; it's human to feel angry at a time like this."

### Emotional Problems and Reactions

One of the feelings the child may be suffering from after a suicide is guilt. In one case, Andrew's father left a suicide note saying he couldn't go on living because he was so upset about his son's involvement with drugs. Naturally, the boy was left with the overwhelming sense that he was responsible for his father's death. "Look, this is really tough," psychiatrist Hal Fishkin told him, "but you weren't the only stressor in your father's life. He was unraveling, and the final part of his unraveling was his killing himself. It must be hard for you. If I were in your shoes, I'd feel awful."

When you're dealing with that kind of guilt, all of the experts agree that it's extremely important to let the child know that if a person really wanted to kill himself, there's nothing anyone could have done to stop him; somehow he would have found a way. "But if only I had picked up on the signs that he was going to do this!" the child is probably thinking. "If only I had been there I could have stopped him!" Let him know that much of the time, those closest to a suicide are the most surprised. So often we hear, "She was the last person in the world I would have expected to do that."

Anger is another emotion that's naturally associated with death. A person usually feels angry when someone he loves dies. But with other kinds of death, the anger can be easily directed against something, vented outward. "That horrible cancer!" "Those dumb doctors!" "That insane murderer!" With suicide the anger is sometimes tougher to direct; it tends to bounce all over—at the dead person's friends, at the other members of the family, at the professional counselor.

Let the child vent that anger, but make sure it's aimed in the right direction—at the person who killed himself. It is natural and healthy to feel angry at being abandoned by a loved one who has committed suicide. Psychiatrist Bruce Danto suggests that one way to help direct that anger is by letting older children read the suicide note, if there is one. Then they'll know the facts. If they don't, they may imagine them to be different. With honest information about what happened, the suicide can be handled in a straightforward, factual manner. That will help keep the youngster in touch with reality, and show the desperation or confusion of the person who died. "Look, you have a right to read this and be angry. Being angry at someone you love doesn't mean that you don't love them." Reassure the child that you will not abandon him in this way: "Don't worry; I would never do that to you. I would never kill myself. I'm really angry at him because he dumped on us. He was a desperate man, he couldn't see any other way out."

Danto stresses the importance of telling the child that the person who committed suicide chose the *wrong way* to solve his problems. Other people have problems and they don't kill themselves. Don't glorify the dead person—make a therapeutic split between him and the survivors. "It takes more courage to live. That he opted for a different way out was his fault." By talking in this way, Danto says you help the child mobilize his anger against the dead person, getting the grieving process started.

Besides guilt and anger, children will also probably have to cope with the stigma associated with suicide. Many of us have been told since childhood that people who commit suicide go to hell. Others assume that the person was crazy, and that the rest of the family must be too. The family members who are left are traumatized, their stability shaken.

When someone in the family commits suicide, a child gets several different messages. One concerns his or her own worth. "I am not lovable enough for him to have hung around for." A second perceived message may be that he or she is a loser, says Bruce Danto. "The child may feel he is being told, 'Look kid, I couldn't make it and neither can you.'" Danto notes that when you break the news to a child that a person he loved has committed suicide, you have to change these perceived messages around so that the child can regain a sense of his own self-worth.

In an article published in *The New York Times*, journalist Lisa Bergson, whose mother committed suicide when she was seven years old, talked about how her brother felt as he tried to resume life in the house they had shared with their mother. "I was no longer a normal kid," he said. "It's like you're a bit of a freak because of what's happened in your family."

Sometimes there are cases where, for one reason or another, a suicide is not labeled as such. Families who are certain that the death was a suicide and who choose to conceal this from their children should be aware of the risks involved. David Peretz, a psychiatrist at Columbia University in New York, points out a couple of these risks. The children may overhear conversations, get a sense that they are not being told the whole story, and then create their own fantasies about what happened. Also, they may find out years later that they have been lied to about this matter of great importance, and then wonder what other lies they've been told. Dr. Peretz says, "It's hard enough to deal with a child when we *know* what he thinks, but when we don't know what he thinks it's almost impossible."

Whether the suicide was intentional or sub-intentional — whether the person was aware at the time that he was actually killing himself or not — it is vitally important that parents convince their children how wrong it was. As we know, a child often models his behavior after that of his parents and others around him, and the evidence is clear that this "modeling" is particularly strong in cases of suicide. I have personally dealt with five cases that were almost the exact duplicates of the suicides of relatives. In one instance, not only were the same site and method used, but it took place at the same hour and on the same day.

A man I know whose father had jumped off a building five years before came in to make arrangements for his brother, who had just done the same thing. Tortured and devastated, he asked me, "Is this the way my family's supposed to die?" This "follow the leader" syndrome is sometimes rooted in romanticism, sometimes in certain feelings of destiny. Whatever the root, it's a connection that must be broken, with discussion, love, and in many cases, therapy.

## Suicides of Children

When a young child thinks of killing himself, he often thinks that suicide is just a temporary thing. Not aware of the finality of death, he sees it as an immediate solution to his problems, or an ultimate punishment for his parents. With the pre-adolescent, suicide may be triggered when the child is abused, depressed, or rejected. Magical thinking takes over, and he may believe that he will be rescued later, like Snow White was. When a teenager commits suicide, however, the reasons are usually much more complicated.

According to Jane Brody, writing in *The New York Times*, the suicide rate among young people under nineteen years of age has increased by about 300 percent since the 1950s. Each day, an average of 18 adolescents kill themselves. Besides the reasons I've already described for suicide, young people have the added burdens of growing up in a transient society, in which upwardly mobile parents often don't take the time to talk with their children about their problems. Widespread use of drugs and alcohol often alter youngsters' senses of reality and help push them on the way to self-destruction. The rash of teenage suicides in the Dallas suburb of Plano and in New York's Westchester County in the past few years prompted many people to take a closer look at the problem and try to do something about it. As I mentioned earlier, courses on death and dying have been set up in a number of high schools and colleges around the country. Openness in talking about suicide removes some of the magic and mystery that teenagers find so appealing; it also helps break the impulse to "follow the leader."

Try to handle suicide as conventionally as possible, mourning it as you would any other death, with a funeral and open grieving for the dead person. This will take away some of the horror and stigma. If you allow a child to go to the funeral home, to talk about the dead person, and look at him and touch him if he wants to, he'll be better able to confront the death and start to grieve. As with other deaths, putting a note in the casket or bringing a good-bye present may help him to "make amends." The child will probably be feeling a lack of security, so he should be told as soon as possible that he will be taken care of, who will be taking care of him, and that he's going to be safe and loved.

Pretending that the person never existed, or that the harm done to the family is so devastating that the person should never be talked about again, will only do more harm to the survivors, especially the children. They need to know that trust exists in the family, no matter what trauma they've been through. As always, talking about the situation and how everyone feels about it will help the family to better cope with the crisis.

## AIDS

The news that a family member has been diagnosed with AIDS is heartbreaking. Equally difficult to deal with is the stigma surrounding the illness, and, often, an anger stemming from the fact that the disease (excepting those who were infected via blood transfusion) is related to a sexual or drug-oriented lifestyle. In many cases, such lifestyles are not easily accepted, or even discussed, among adult family members. It is all the more difficult to discuss them with children.

As I've said before, kids today can't be fooled. We must think of the effect upon them when they see one thing, but are told something else—or nothing at all. The decision of what, when, and how much to say rests ultimately with the parent or caregiver, but to say nothing usually backfires.

The intense anger experienced by some AIDS survivors, which may be directed at either the deceased or his or her lifestyle choices, can be spoken about among adults. But it can be confusing for children. (You may wish to consult the observations on anger in the Crisis Checklist.)

The massive exposure given to AIDS in the media may well help curb the spread of the disease. But I have seen another effect as well: a heightened consciousness and fear among children.

"When my father had a mild heart attack and was hospitalized," Joan said, "my eight-year-old wanted to know if grandpa had AIDS. I guess it was a good thing she asked, though. She might have not said anything, and just worried about mommy and daddy and her contracting AIDS. Or she might have thought that grandpa was a drug addict or a homosexual."

Some adults have difficulty with their own concerns about AIDS and how it's transmitted. Not everyone is comforted by assurances from the medical field based on current research. Even well informed adults can feel at risk from casual contact, and have difficulty reassuring their children. As in any other situation, though, we can go only by the resources we have at hand. And so, as the number of AIDS cases increases, we look forward to a greater effort at education, and we encourage compassionate and open communication.

AIDS is a saga that continues to unfold. The dramatic increase in the number of people with HIV/AIDS and the diversity of those affected have brought new challenges to the caregiving community and greater attention to the wider issue of how our culture treats its bereaved. The impact of HIV/AIDS clearly requires empathy and understanding and the creation of a truly nurturing community.

When the AIDS epidemic began, the focus of caregivers was on the HIV/AIDS patient, but it soon became evident that HIV/AIDS also greatly affects the children, siblings, parents, friends, lovers, spouses, and caregivers of patients. The scope of caregiving had to be expanded beyond medical treatment for the patient to psychological and social therapy for the patient and his/her community.

Dealing with children and AIDS is especially painful. Michael Lipson, Ph.D., a Senior Psychologist in Harlem Hospital's Department of Pediatrics, describes some of the difficulties. "Parents are ripped out of their roles as parents. When a parent is the one diagnosed with HIV/AIDS she may feel she is abandoning her children and forsaking her role as a parent. It is a very nonparental thing to do, to leave a child."

## Parents with AIDS

One of the greatest concerns for parents with AIDS is how their illness will affect their children. Carol Cohen, R.N., is a member of a team of caregivers at Lutheran Medical Center in Brooklyn, New York, which meets with HIV/AIDS patients and their families to help them sort through this difficult issue. Their work, which has been recognized by the Southern Medical Association, assists HIV-positive parents in planning for the future of their HIV-negative children. These parents have many questions about how their illness will affect their children. Who will care for the children when the parent is in the hospital? Who will disclose the diagnosis and prognosis to the children? When and how should they be told? What will be the impact on the children? How will their community, school, and peers respond to them? What about long-term care? Should children be tested for HIV? What if they too are positive?

The complexity of the issues clearly requires early intervention by a diverse team of caregivers. They can help reduce some of the patient's stress and concerns about planning and caring for their children. It is important to resolve these matters early on because of the risk of the parent being unable to participate as the illness progresses. More than half of AIDS patients experience loss of mental functions, making communication difficult.

## What Children Know

Children know when there is a secret in the family and when they are being left out. They read family emotions, overhear conversations, hear neighbors talk, and see changes taking place as the patient's disease progresses. Still, in AIDS cases many people choose not to volunteer information to children, or if questioned, not to reply. Dr. Lipson of Harlem Hospital admits that this is a very delicate matter, but feels that those who know earlier do better over the long term. For a mother to say, "I'm dying," is an admission of her mortality and of the impending loss for her family. This does not happen easily. "But what's really significant," he says, "is that the truth will come out; not talking only worsens the inevitable. A parent should have the opportunity to talk to her child, hug, cry, and face the pain."

Psychotherapist Ruth Rothbart-Mayer asks adults to think of their own childhood. "What did you want to know? How did you feel if you were left out?" As has been emphasized, when we were little most of us liked being included in all the activities around us. Carol Cohen says, "It's our experience with the children we see at Lutheran Medical Center that they seem relieved when their suspicions are confirmed. When I meet with the families of HIV and AIDS patients, I explain that in my children's groups, I will not lie about a patient's diagnosis. I won't disclose without permission from the family, but I won't lie. Sometimes this is so frightening to family members that they refuse to bring the children back."

Karen's husband became quite ill with pneumonia. Should we check for AIDS? No! He didn't fit the profile, but he did have AIDS. He was reasonably healthy for almost a year except for a worsening cough. In fact, he worked until about a week before he died. "I raged at the disease and my husband for leaving me, for abandoning me. I raged at everything," Karen admitted. "I was in the ozone. My daughter was three and a half. It must have been so confusing for her. I know my personality went out the window. My daughter was too young for AIDS information, and I couldn't talk about it without rage. I was really too angry and upset to talk."

Did her daughter know? Looking back, Karen says her daughter knew one thing: that she had been shut out. She was "shut out of the discussions I had with my husband. Our place was pretty big and we tried to shut a door to talk or we spelled a lot. We were surprised to overhear her play acting out with her dolls one of our family scenes including our 'secrets.' "

## How to Tell

There can be no cookie-cutter approach to explaining to a child that someone is dying. To help parents talk to their children, Rothbart-Mayer suggests they first confront their own worries. "What are you worried will happen if you talk about what's going on?" Perhaps your response will be one of the following: "My kids won't go to school." "Kids will make fun of her." "She'll cry a lot." "She'll pout." "He'll act out or be depressed." Rothbart-Mayer says that some people feel talking will hasten death. Whatever the individual concerns are, the parent with AIDS should first examine his or her own feelings, build some emotional stability, and deal with feelings of betrayal, anger, and abandonment, and then approach the children.

Cohen and her team at the Lutheran Medical Center try to encourage communication about the disease and the fears and concerns of the family while the patient is still in good physical and mental condition. Parents seem to feel better if a trained outsider talks to their children. Whether in a group or alone, children usually talk more freely with Cohen's team than with family members.

The team method involves several steps. First, they pull the children out of school and try to find out where they are at. Then they find out how they feel about mom or dad being sick and in the hospital. Older children in groups seem to do all the talking, so the children are often split up to give the little ones a chance to talk.

Dr. Lipson suggests telling the oldest child first, in the most understandable terms, bit by bit, not all at once. Sharing this extremely painful information with a child must be a slow, merciful process.

Barbara Dane, D.S.W., a psychotherapist and associate professor at New York University's School of Social Work, points out that most children will have questions about the parent's illness. One way to answer these questions is to involve them in the caregiving process. She suggests taking them to the doctor. "It's a beginning for the parent to answer typical questions, such as 'Mommy what does the doctor do?' and 'What about all these other people, new people, who come to our house, what do they do? What's a visiting nurse? What's a nutritionist?' "

Be prepared to deal with the special concerns a child might have. Young children ask, "Who will take care of me?" This is a common reaction for a young child when a parent dies.

"What if something happens to my surviving parent?" This issue is of greater concern in families where both parents are ill and a child sees only an aging grandparent as a potential caregiver. Teens have additional concerns. "If I have children, will this happen again?"

Some people rush to tell everything, to get it all out. Is how the person contracted the disease important? To many people it is. It may not be important to your child. Before you say anything, ask yourself, "How angry am I?" If you are angry, it's probably not the time to talk about it. One mother is withholding information about her husband's disease from their child not so much because the information will shame the child but because she fears the child's anger at having been shut out so long.

"This is very delicate information," says Rothbart-Mayer. "I think there is a part of the story children have to come to themselves. How the person got AIDS, for example. Some kids say they don't want to know, particularly if it's embarrassing."

Many families don't want to confront the issue of previous lifestyles. They fear the reaction of their children and in turn the reaction of their children's friends. This is particularly true in areas where these lifestyles were covert.

It is important to remember though that while talking is necessary and therapeutic, it can be heartbreaking. A good example is this conversation between a dying mother and her infant: "I'm leaving. I am so sad. I never meant it to be this way. I never meant to leave you. I'm going to make sure you are cared for and taken care of."

One of the greatest benefits of being candid with children is that the children feel free to share their own feelings. Karen's words to her grandfather were, "I hope you're not dying but if you are, thanks for being so nice to me, and taking me great places, and teaching me to fish and paint. Thanks for loving me."

### Children's Reactions

When you tell a child something this traumatic, don't expect a response right away. In addition, don't expect an adult response from a child. "Sometimes," says Dane, "it takes time for a child to process the information. One mother told her eleven-year-old son that his father was dying. "He just stared at me, waited a while, and walked away. Only four days later was he ready to ask for more information and talk about it."

Accepting a child's timing and waiting can be difficult and confusing for an adult. "What's the matter with them?" frustrated parents ask. "Why don't they say something?" According to Dr. Dane, "Kids hear what you say and then they shut down. It's a way to cope with shock and trauma. Some children, like some adults, take longer than others. Tough as it is, adults should try to be ready to respond when the child is ready to ask."

## Family Privacy and Community Reaction

When someone has been diagnosed with HIV/AIDS, complex issues arise concerning who should be told. Families must deal with reactions that range from fear to panic, from misinformation to discrimination. Caregivers point out that in deaths from cancer, suicide, or accidents, people react strongly at first but gradually the reaction begins to dissipate. With AIDS, however, people seem to continue to react. Some say they never stop reacting.

Caregivers point to privacy as an important issue to address with children. Rothbart-Mayer stresses the difference between family privacy and stigma. Family privacy is information that does not need to leave the family. Rothbart-Mayer says that the real issue is self-protection and protection of your child. You must decide when it's important for someone to know and then ask, "If you tell this person, how will it help? Do you think the person will still be your friend? We have suffered a terrible loss, but we want to maintain our family, so we want to keep talking."

Rothbart-Mayer suggests the following approach might help: "When I was little I didn't realize how much I hated being left out. There have been things your daddy and I didn't tell you. Now you are old enough so that if I tell you that something is private to our family, you will appreciate that."

"Daddy has a disease in his blood. It's a new disease and people don't have a good feeling about it. It makes them afraid. Be very careful who you tell or talk to because some people don't understand."

People in an effort not to disclose information sometimes choose the wrong people not to tell. Schools need to know what's going on. Look for an "anchor person," someone who would be sensitive and who the child could go to if he or she wanted to talk. Teachers or supervisors need to be prepared if they are going to help.

Rothbart-Mayer points out the importance of the doctor being aware of the child's thought process. A mother whose husband was battling AIDS took her son to the doctor for a fever. The doctor told the child that he had a virus. He knew that his daddy had a virus but a very big one. The doctor's diagnosis frightened the child. "Mommy, do I have a virus like daddy? Will I get as sick as daddy?" Mom had to explain to the doctor how specific he had to be with her son. The doctor explained, "Your daddy has a very, very big virus and yours is a very tiny virus. It's a different virus."

## HOW TO TALK TO CHILDREN ABOUT SOMEONE WHO IS DYING

Pat stood with his father outside his mother's room at a Manhattan hospital. During his sophomore year in college, Pat remembers as if it were yesterday the doctor leaving his mother's room, coming up to his father, and saying, "Your wife has about twenty minutes." Twenty-five years later the memory is still vivid. "It didn't register at first. I remember saying to my father, 'Twenty minutes for what?' I knew my mother was sick but no one told me how serious her illness was."

Now a high-school guidance counselor, Pat acknowledges how difficult it must have been for his father, but still recalls the feelings of anger and bitterness at the "protection" he was given by his family. "I had no opportunity to say the things I wanted to say. No chance to tell her I loved her. No chance to say good-bye. If only [my father] had had some advice. If only he had thought about me." Over and over caregivers hear painful stories such as this one from children and adults.

There is no easy way to tell a child that someone he loves is dying. At the request of parents and caregivers we offer the following information and advice gathered from children and parents, in addition to a wide range of helpers. We sincerely hope that their words, based on experience, will make the task easier for you.

## What Children Want to Know

"We want honesty!" says one fourteen-year-old. "Parents skirt around the issue. You can really see how uncomfortable adults are when they try to talk to children. My father was missing from his boat for two days before they found his body. They never told me. It made me feel like I wasn't important enough to know. They thought I couldn't handle it but I could have, if only they had told me. It really makes me angry and it was four years ago."

Professionals agree that children are a lot stronger than one might guess. Ruth Rothbart-Mayer, M.S.W, C.S.W, a psychotherapist and cofounder of the Mayer-Avedon Women's Support Group in New York City, asks adults to recall their own childhood. "When you were a child, what did you want to know? How did you feel when you were left out?" Most of us liked being included, we liked being asked.

Recounting his father's illness 13-year-old Glen remembers, "I wanted to be told everything but no one would talk to me." Donna Schuurman, Executive Director of the

Dougy Center, a childhood bereavement center in Portland, Oregon, says, "I've never met a kid who said, 'I wish they lied to me.' Carl, a fourteen-year-old talking about the death of his father, confirms this: "I don't know which is worse, outright lies or these fabrications that adults make up. I don't know if they think we don't see what's happening around us."

Dysfunction and alienation can be created by sending mixed messages. Robby agrees: "I saw what was happening, but they were telling me something different. It was very confusing." Schuurman adds, "Children learn quickly to shut up when the adult message is 'we're not talking about this'."

Lying may be referred to euphemistically as "protecting the child." Children say that they are better able to understand and also handle tough situations than most people give them credit for. "There is enough pain and hurt going on already," Chris said. "I don't know why they have to add lies on top of it all. just tell us the truth." He added that if someone just said they didn't know how to talk about dying, that would have been a start. "Then at least we'd be together knowing we were hurting and upset, and I wouldn't be left alone."

### Children Take a Back Seat

Occasionally parents, overwhelmed by caring for a sick family member, are so upset and focused on the sick person that children are forced to take a back seat and often are neglected, sometimes for years. "I didn't realize until ten years after my son's death, while attending a conference, that I was so absorbed with my loss and my grief that I was really nothing to my daughter. I sat there as this tremendous wave of guilt swept over me. I had gone inside myself and stayed there," says Susan, whose thirteen-year-old son had died ten years prior.

"Maybe we could put something in writing," said Kelly, "to let our parents know what it's like when we become invisible."

### A Neutral Party

Mike's wife is very ill, but he isn't ready to acknowledge just how serious the situation is. "I'm really hoping that my wife will get well," says Mike. "I don't want someone telling my kid how serious this is and scaring him." His ten-year-old son Tim can see his mother's condition getting worse. His problem is that what he is being told doesn't match what he is seeing.

Often dealing with your own feelings and emotions, giving everything you have to a sick family member, and trying to maintain some semblance of order in your own life leave you short of the mental energy to communicate effectively with your children. In these situations the intercession of a neutral party can be helpful.

A neutral party can be anyone who is not intimately involved with the dynamics of the family. The best candidate is a mental health professional who can bridge the gaps among family members. A trained therapist will listen to the child's concerns, validate what the child sees, and then bring these concerns back to the parent. A therapist might report to Mike, in the case cited above, "Your child believes his mother is very sick. Tim is afraid his mother is going to die. Tim is afraid you might get as sick as your wife and that you may die."

I wouldn't rule out a well-meaning neighbor or friend as

a neutral party, but one must be careful. A trained therapist, without divulging anything harmful to the child, can help position the parent to be the one who can best guide the child. I'm not sure a well-meaning neighbor or friend can accomplish that. If your child had a toothache or a broken arm, you would seek treatment from a trained professional. The same care should be taken in selecting a neutral party.

## Regrets at Waiting Too Long

"We knew our son Tommy was dying. Inside we knew, but we did everything we could to keep him busy, to divert him from 'it.' When he lapsed into a coma a week before he died we talked to him. We all felt he heard us, but we desperately wanted a response we would never get." Now these parents say they should have spoken sooner. "We had been encouraged to speak sooner by the social workers in the hospital, but we said no," John acknowledged. "Maybe if we had talked to a parent who had 'been there,' who had had the same experience, we would have acted differently."

Erica Leeuwenburgh, M.P.S., A.T.R., Supervisor of Creative Art Therapy/Child Life Services at Hackensack Medical Center's Tomorrow's Children's Institute in Hackensack, New Jersey, makes an important observation about hope and denial. "Many people feel that you can't be hopeful and still talk about your fears. The fears are there, so talking about them is important; denying them doesn't make them go away."

Twelve-year-old Lynn's experience confirms this. She remembers: "It was so hard to say good-bye to my brother, but now I just couldn't imagine not being there with him and sharing the things we shared."

Families that know and acknowledge that a person is dying don't need to talk about it every day, but once the subject is broached it frees them to talk about a lot of other related matters. Is this important? Studies conclude that communication is beneficial. It helps the dying person to talk to family members about his or her thoughts and concerns, and thereby assists family members to relinquish their feelings of regret. Feelings of sadness, grief, pain, or depression are unavoidable, but regret can be alleviated. Family members say that as tough as it may be, it was better once feelings were openly discussed, than carrying around the "I wish I saids" for the rest of their lives.

## I Just Don't Know What to Say

You don't have to have all the answers. "How can I take care of myself, deal with all that is happening, and also respond positively to my child?" a parent asks. "My daughter asks me question after question. Sometimes I think I'm going to explode."

A therapist advises, "Get some space. Create some boundaries. You need to be safe too."

"But how do I stay in there with my child and also create space?"

You might try some of these responses: "Mommy doesn't have the answer to that question right now," or "Mommy doesn't know how to answer that question right now, but I'll try to find an answer for you." A different approach might be: "Talking about that right now makes Daddy very sad. Give me a little while and maybe then we can talk about it." Or you might say, "I can see you're very concerned about that. Give me a while and then we can talk." If in the middle of a conversation you become upset, you might say,

"Daddy doesn't feel comfortable talking about this any-more. We have to stop for a while." Rothbart-Mayer adds, "Make sure you keep your word and come back to your child's question, as difficult as it may be."

Both you and your child need a place that feels safe. This approach allows that without pushing the child away. It keeps communication open for future talks and lets children know that it's okay for them to talk and stop, talk and stop, when it's too much for them. It creates a very respecting environment. Parents don't have to say everything and can still respond to the child's questions.

Simply saying, "Don't worry. Everything will be okay," isn't a good solution. Does the child see in you a person who really thinks things will be okay? Does he see you acting like things are getting better? Probably not. This response or ones like it just throw a blanket over reality.

## Adults Talking to Children

When talking to children, don't expect a response immediately. Children live in the here and now. They may hear now, but not respond until some time later. Rothbart-Mayer uses a traffic light as a model for talking with a child. Red light means stop. If a child says stop, then stop. Let them know you will be there when they are ready. Children don't need to be told more than they want to know. A yellow light means proceed with caution. A green light is a go-ahead. This may not be easy to pick up, but being aware that the child controls the lights is very important to recognize.

Carol was concerned about her planned summer visit to Germany. She was taking her twelve-year-old daughter for their annual visit to her grandmother. Carol had heard from her sister that her mother had been diagnosed with terminal cancer. It was now November. What should she say to her daughter? Should she continue with her plans? She was concerned about what condition her mother would be in by June and how her daughter would be affected by the change. Carol wondered if she should discuss the whole impact of her mother's diagnosis with her daughter, including the feelings she had about losing her mother.

I suggested that Carol take it one day at a time, offering medical reports as she received them. "Today Grandma isn't feeling very well. I'm concerned, and we will have to see how she is feeling tomorrow." This day-to-day strategy worked well for her. "When I felt sad I was able to explain that to my daughter and she could understand. It felt great and not great at the same time. Also, she was able to talk to me. She didn't have to feel that she had to protect me, as so many kids attempt to do."

Communicating the impact of a serious illness to someone else is very difficult indeed. The Reverend Jack Stouffer, CoDirector with the Reverend Maury Drumm of Pastoral Care at Lutheran Medical Center in Brooklyn, New York, says, "You can almost see the numbness set into the family. At times there is almost a total screening of what's happening. It's like they slip into a twilight zone of reality. Sometimes I wonder if what we're saying gets in at all."

The stoplight model can be helpful at times like these. "Mary is very sick, and I'm very concerned." Yellow light. "I really don't know what's coming in the future." Yellow light. "I have some sincere doubts about her getting well." Sharing how you feel and where you are right now seems to be a thread that has connected many of the people I've spoken to.

"I don't want to come right out and say 'he's dying,' " Liz said. "No matter how I try to get the message across to Sue, it's not getting through. It's almost like she doesn't want to hear it or believe it and she just shuts me off."

What can or should you do about denial? Ken Moses, Ph.D., clinical psychologist with Resource Network in Evanston, Illinois, sees denial as a person's way of buying time to mobilize internal coping mechanisms and organize external support systems needed to face the facts, implications, and feelings associated with loss. However, if denial continues, some professional help may be necessary to help a person begin the grieving process.

## Secrets

Secrets are a myth. They really don't exist. Both professional caregivers and children say almost everyone knows the secret. The message is definitely getting out. Is it the message that you want? Here are some questions to ask yourself:

- What do my children know already?
- What have they overheard? (If you want your children to hear everything you say, go three rooms away and whisper.)
- What do my children understand of what they see and hear?
- What do my children hear outside our home?
- What happens to them at school?
- What do they pick up from the media?
- What are my children's fears and concerns?
- Do I want an inside kid or an outside kid? (An inside kid has been brought into a family support system.

An outside kid has been placed outside the family support system with very little information.)
- Is my child trying to protect me?
- Will it be easier for me to communicate with my child while help is around or by myself later?
- How will I answer the question: Why didn't you tell me?

### The Child as Protector

A child may rationalize, "If I talk about this, my parents will get upset or even cry. I don't want to be responsible for making them feel bad, so I won't talk about this thing that's happening."

All too often, parents, unaware of what is really happening, will conclude that a child who doesn't voice his or her anxieties is "doing just fine." If a child seems undisturbed by the serious illness of a family member, he or she may be trying to protect you from additional anxiety. You may want to talk more openly about your feelings and how normal they are under the circumstances. "When someone is as sick as Uncle Dan, most people get really upset. We worry about him and about whether he will get better." This may give your child the opening to talk about his or her concerns.

### Children, Fear, and Art

Sometimes children who find it difficult to communicate verbally are able to illustrate what they're afraid of through drawings. Art is a tool therapists use to help children express their fears. The therapists at the Outreach Program at Hackensack Children's Hospital, for example, have had good success with this technique. "We were treating a child from a small tight-knit community who was clearly going to die. The parents of his friends asked us to meet with their children to see if we could help," team member Judy Solomon, M. S. W., C. S. W., remembers. "The parents didn't want their children to be dealing with this loss alone over the summer or have to confront their friend's absence at the school-bus stop in September. The parents and the staff felt that this would save a lot of pain. We met with the children in the home of one of the parents. We found that through illustrating their fears and then talking about their drawings they were able to come to terms with the impending death of their friend."

Children may not start with words. It may be easier on them if they are in control of communicating their feelings without being questioned. Drawing allows children to communicate their observations to caregivers. Margaret Zamierowski, M.P.S., Bereavement Coordinator of Brooklyn Hospice, describes working with a family in turmoil over a serious family crisis. As a trained art therapist, she asked the children to draw a picture of the family. To her amazement all five children drew a picture of a house on fire. By asking children what's going on in their pictures, some clues about the children's perceptions of what they see around them are revealed. Hackensack Medical Center's Leeuwenburgh and Solomon point out that what is important is not the drawing itself, but what it means to the child. You are not only analyzing the drawing, but rather using the drawing as a bridge to communication.

Many parents say that through the course of the illness they wished they had kept an album or video of some of the happy events that they experienced with their child, both at the hospital and at home. Some parents talk about the need to have photographs or videos of some of the "crazy" moments, such as parties and gatherings with families and friends. It helps them to remember that the times weren't all bad.

## School

Beth Evans, an educator and consultant to schools on crisis and bereavement in Spring Valley, New York, speaks of the importance and value of a child's school in the family support system. She recalls hearing that a student's mother had been given six months to live. "I had the sense that something was going on. The child was definitely in distress, fighting, acting out, lacking concentration, and performing far below her capability. As it turns out," says Evans, "the child's father was not acknowledging that his wife was truly dying. We could have helped, if we had more time. Maybe we could have pointed out to the father the effect this was having on his daughter, then perhaps referred him to a mental health professional, and assisted with the assurance of continued support. As it happened the illness accelerated, and we only had two weeks."

Informing schools is critically important. They can be an incredible resource, providing information for your child and helping strengthen your child's support system by working with his or her peers. Evans recalls a school spelling bee where a teacher asked a student to spell the word "party." The teacher said, "I asked Tommy to spell 'party' because Friday is his birthday and he will be having a party." "No party on Friday," Tommy replied. "My mommy died this morning." Both the teacher and the child's classmates were shocked. Some knew that the child's mother was sick, but the seriousness of her condition was a family secret, and we've been taught never to tell family secrets.

Back-to-school nights and special school seminars are opportunities to show parents how special circumstances within a family affect children at school, and to reassure them that the school is able to intervene and be sensitive to the long-range effects of loss. A strong community alliance like this can create a nurturing environment for children and all those who grieve.

## HOW TO TALK TO A MENTALLY RETARDED CHILD

The loss of a loved one can affect someone who is mentally retarded, though it may be harder to discern the impact on such a person. People tend to try to protect mentally retarded children and adults or to spare them from upsetting events. A death may be denied and the impact of a loss minimized. Even when it's acknowledged, children and adults with mental retardation may not be told what is going on, may not be allowed to participate in rituals such as the wake or funeral, and may not be encouraged to display their grief.

Constance Butherus, R.N., M.A., Director of Professional and Residential Services at the Hunterdon Developmental Center in Clinton, New Jersey, describes their program. Under appropriate circumstances, patients are involved in a hospice setting at their residence. They see their friend's illness, much as people would at home. There is an opportunity for the staff to assist with their adjustments to the changes that the illness brings, to help with care, and to experience the loss as a family.

Butherus explains, "We chose to err on the side of providing more information rather than less. Our staff becomes the surrogate family. We feel that the ideal person to communicate with the patient is the caregiver closest to the patient. But death is not the only loss our patients experience. Moving to a different residence or an absent staff member can upset patients, so we are very sensitive to their feelings and adjustments."

Support for families of a mentally retarded person is essential, and it can come in many forms. Caregivers can help a family understand the normal grief reactions. They can prepare families for the resistance of others who feel the mentally retarded family member should not be included. They can help the family find a model for appropriate behavior. And, finally, they can provide factual information and opportunities for communication.

A professional caregiver can also identify a mentally retarded person who is acting out in response to the loss, and assist with the grieving process, thus easing the family's adjustment.

Sharing information with someone who is mentally retarded should be a gradual process. Start with the most basic information and proceed to a level where you determine that the mentally retarded person is beginning to understand. If the death of a parent is involved, don't forget to deal with the issues of continued care.

Jeffrey Kauffman, M.A., Director of the Center for the Care of Community Institutions in St. Peters, Pennsylvania, suggests that helping the family prepare their mentally retarded family member for the death of a primary caregiver beforehand may help reduce the anxiety of the family and the severe trauma often experienced by a mentally retarded person who is not adequately prepared.

## DEATH OF A PET

The death of a pet can cause pain that is deep and enduring, yet easy to underestimate. Many people forget that a pet is like a member of the family, so the pain caused by its loss—whether experienced by a child or an adult—should not be ignored or minimized. By making well-intentioned comments such as "It's only a cat. You can always get another one," family members may seem unsympathetic, and may force the grieving pet owners to deal with their loss without support.

Beth Evans, an expert on bereavement working in the school system in Spring Valley, New York, uses an example of a sixth-grader whose dog died while the child was away at camp. During camp visits throughout the summer his parents did not mention the dog's death. Five years later, he describes his feelings: "By the end of camp I was really very anxious to get back to my dog. When I walked in the door I was greeted with the news that the dog was dead. Why didn't they tell me when it happened?"

A friend shares a similar story: "My parents said they sent the dog to Florida. 'It's nice there and he'll have a good home.' " Many years later she discovered that the dog had been put down. "I felt so betrayed and hurt. I couldn't believe that they would lie to me. I began to wonder what other lies they told me."

Barbara Meyers, Director of the Holistic Animal Consulting Center, Staten Island, New York, reminds us that in dealing with grief for an animal the issue is not the animal but the bereaved one's feelings. "It's about respect for the loss. Where children are concerned, listen to their feelings and respect their grief. No matter how you feel about their pet, the issue is how they feel about it." The relationship between a companion animal and its owner is a unique and irreplaceable one. Meyers points out, "No paw has ever jerked away from a deformed human hand that reaches for it. The open display of physical affection has never been withdrawn because the object of that affection has become sick, old, or unattractive."

 Make sure the child understands that the death of an animal is very different from that of a human being. If a pet needs to be killed, don't use the term "put to sleep." Instead, explain that the pet had to be killed in order to end its suffering. At the same time, make clear that we don't do that with people. If the death of a pet is handled well—if the child is told exactly what is happening to the animal and why, and if he or she is given the opportunity to remember the pet with a backyard "burial service," or perhaps just with long discussions of the good times they had together and how bad it feels—then it can give you a starting point for any future encounters with death.

# 3

## Grief and Healing

Seventeen-year-old Amy sat in the parlor car of the train, looking out the window and going over every minute of the last few days in her mind. Her sister and mother sat across from her, absorbed in their books. But Amy could do nothing but stare out the window and listen to the beat of the train against the tracks. Her mind was frozen with anxiety.

Back in Memphis, in a grave not yet marked with a stone, lay her grandmother. She had been quite a lady—a poet, a gardener, a gentlewoman—and to Amy, a kind and sensitive best friend to talk to. Only six people had shown up at the funeral, and as the young priest stood on the altar behind the casket, he intoned words that would stick in Amy's mind for a lifetime. "Everyone is precious in God's eyes— the great and famous, and the little people like Margaret here, who go about their lives quietly, never making much of an impression, never seeming to make much of a difference. . . . The words went around and around in Amy's head as she tried to make some sense out of it all; all the while rage was growing inside her. Her grandmother was important, she *did* make a difference. The world was a better place because of her!

In Amy's family, people didn't talk about their feelings. That kind of thing was dismissed as sentimental and self-indulgent. Actions were more important than words. If something bothered you, you worked it out yourself. So, Amy's pain and resentment smoldered inside her for months. She never cried. A couple of years later it all burst forth in a severe depression. Fortunately, she had a boyfriend who was sensitive and a good listener; he helped her to heal.

Teenagers, young children, adults . . . everyone needs a release valve, someone to be the catalyst to help them work their feelings out. Without this catalyst, a wall is built up around the grieving person. Sometimes, as in Amy's case, we do much of the construction ourselves. Amy's mother didn't even know the wall was there. But very often, especially in the case of small children, the parents do the handiwork, creating a sturdy barrier that they think will protect their child from pain.

This wall tends to be made of fairy tales, incomplete messages, suppressed emotions. Does it do the job parents expect it to? Maybe, in the case of infants, it does. But professionals agree that once a child is over the age of two or three, it isn't an effective strategy. Step on the other side of the wall and take a look at your child. Do you see a youngster who's relatively happy or one who's really upset? It could be that he or she is confused, or grieving, and not getting enough support. That's a problem that can certainly be remedied, now that you are equipped with the right tools.

In this chapter we will look at the ways in which children cope with death and grief, and see how you can help the healing process. Again, let me remind you that you might not find the exact answer to your situation outlined here, be-

cause each situation is unique. I hope you will take what applies to you and work it into your family blueprint.

Sometimes parents come in and ask me to talk to their
children myself, to explain death to them, and I always tell
the parents the same thing. "You are the ones who are with
the children day to day, and it is you they will come to three
months down the road with questions." There is a little saying that applies here: If you give a man a fish, you feed him
for a day; but if you give him a hook and teach him to fish,
you feed him for a lifetime. Certainly, it would be easier if I
or some other outside person did the talking, but it would
be only a temporary relief. Who will answer the questions at
three o'clock in the morning when the child wakes up wondering where Grandpa is? It's difficult watching your child
grieve, but once you've broken down the wall and opened
the channels of communication with your child, you'll
know what to expect, how he'll react, and how to help him.

Start by asking yourself a few questions. First,. how close
was your child to the person who died? If it was just a casual
acquaintance, a neighbor down the street of whom he was
only vaguely aware, the child will probably not be too upset.
But if it was a family member or classmate, someone who
was really a part of his life, the child may be devastated—
not only by the death, but by the fact that the routine of his
life will be in an upheaval. Things will not be going the way
they usually do, and that can be very unsettling for a child.

A second thing to consider is what kind of person the
child is. Children, like adults, have different personalities,
so they grieve differently when they're in a crisis. Some are
stoic, others get hysterical; some withdraw, others throw
themselves into activities; some are philosophical and accepting, others are angry and belligerent. The differences in

reaction are due in part to the way the child has been taught to behave. In each family there are certain patterns of behavior that are acceptable. The members of one family may be demonstrative, warm, and affectionate with each other. In another family, they'll be more reserved.

The child's family background helps give him stability and a framework in which to work out his grief. Most bereavement counselors I've talked to agree, however, that children from demonstrative families have an easier time getting through grief because they've already learned how to show their emotions.

## COMMON REACTIONS
## TO GRIEF

How do children faced with a death express their grief? Here are some typical kinds of behavior.

### Exhaustion

Many children who are experiencing grief for the first time will have physical symptoms like exhaustion. Sixteen-year-old Anne felt as though someone had pulled a plug and drained all her energy out of her. "I can hardly walk up the stairs," she sighed. While she focused her effort on trying to get over her grief, there was less energy left for other things.

Other common reactions are sleeping much of the time ("I just want to make the world go away"); loss of appetite ("I can't eat. The food tastes like sandpaper"); and lethargy ("She just sits there like a bump on a log, doing nothing").

## Dependency

"She won't do anything unless someone else suggests it and actually goes along with her. She can't seem to make decisions. And she used to be so independent!" This need for support in the extreme, where the child becomes very dependent, attaching him or herself to others, is part of the state of disorganization that often accompanies grief. Not able to initiate and maintain their own activities, helpless and afraid of being alone, the children are in a sense reaching out to those around them.

## Feelings of Unreality

In the early days after a death, a number of youngsters have said that they felt as though this were happening to someone else, that they were watching a movie with themselves in it. "Someone who looks like me is standing here. And those people look like my family. But it just can't be!" Feeling empty, alone, and out of control, the child wants to be with the person who died . . . to touch him and sit and talk with him.

One child explained: "It's as though part of *me* has died." The child is still able to function, even go to school or talk with friends, but there is a feeling that he is going about the routine of his life without thinking, filled with a sense of unreality.

## Panic

Afraid that some other devastating thing is going to happen, afraid of being alone at night, afraid of he doesn't even know what, a child may feel a sense of panic as he tries to put the death of the person in perspective and go on with his life. Depressed, vulnerable, tired, and listless, the feelings overwhelm him. "I just don't know what to do," seven-year-old Brendan sobbed. "Nobody can help me, I feel so bad." Fortunately, that little boy had a mother and a sister who sat beside him every night for two weeks while he went through his night terrors. When a child has this sense of panic, this anxiety, he needs to be told that it will pass, that in time he'll be okay and that he'll be able to think about the person who died and not have the pain. He needs to be given hope.

### Preoccupation with the Dead Person

Preoccupation with the person who died is another very common symptom of grief. Everything reminds the child of that person, and in trying to distance himself from his pain, the child may pull away from his friends and family.

> A few weeks after the death of her father, fourteen-year-old Linda just couldn't stop thinking about him. Over and over again, she played the scenes of their times together in her mind. Whenever anyone tried to divert her, she became irritable. She also had difficulty sleeping, and sometimes at two o'clock in the morning you could find her in her room, trying to read herself to sleep. "Sometimes I felt so weird I thought I was going crazy," she remembered. "All I could think about was my daddy and how he was dead."

To identify with the dead person, a child even occasionally starts imitating his actions, walking as he walked, doing things that he might have done. Joseph, a twelve-year-old, became the family handyman after his father died, slipping into the role of Mr. Fix-it just like his father. When a friend came over to help fix the boiler, Joseph went down to the basement with him, all the while giving advice: "This is how my father would do it." Sliding into that role was good for Joseph; he had found his niche. It gave him a little sense of control and helped him find an anchor during the mourning period. Sometimes, though, this imitation and identification can be negative. Meg's grandmother was chronically sick during her whole life. Right after she died, thirteen-year-old Meg, who was very close to her, developed chronic migraine headaches, just like her grandmother. She needed professional help before she got over them.

## Hyperactivity

Some children, as they're mourning, become hyperactive, hopping from thing to thing aimlessly, searching for something to do. In their restlessness they act as though they've been plugged into an electrical socket, and you may look with wonder at them. "Where do they get that energy?" Some children talk incessantly, others laugh when they feel like crying; but no amount of talking or laughing seems to ease their minds.

## Destructive Behavior

One mild-mannered young fellow all of a sudden became hostile and obnoxious when an aunt he adored died. Feeling helpless and full of despair, he lashed out at those around him, completely out of character. When his mother helped him talk his feelings out, he calmed down again. Another child, a ten-year-old who was unable to express his grief after his father died, tried to bring those feelings out in a physical way. Sitting under a table at the memorial service, the boy tugged at the tablecloth, bringing the memorial candle that was sitting on top of the table closer and closer to the edge. This kind of destructive misbehavior is not a common reaction; it's highly unusual, but it points up what can happen in the mind of a child who doesn't know how to talk about what's bothering him. If your child experiences a big behavior change, and it lasts more than a few days, you may need extra help to guide him through his grief.

## Regression

Regression is a common symptom of grief. Six-year-olds who have been toilet trained for years may suddenly revert to wetting the bed. Preteens, usually very much in touch with reality, may slide back into the magical thinking of a preschooler. In one dramatic case, a ten-year-old whose grandmother had died opened the window of his apartment, planning to jump out. Later, when he was asked which way he'd go if he took the leap, the boy said, "Up." Desperately lonely for his grandmother, who had raised him, he regressed into magical thinking and reasoned that by jumping out the window, he'd be reunited with his grandmother, who he believed was up in the clouds, in heaven.

That, of course, is an extreme example, and that child obviously needed extra help to get over his reunification fantasy, his magical thinking, and his pain. But it's clear that children can be severely affected by the death of those close to them. Years ago, it was thought that children were incapable of grief. How wrong that thinking is!

If a child's life is already in turmoil, if he or she is having trouble at home or at school, there will probably be more trouble dealing with the death than if life had been relatively calm. An adult, feeling shaky and vulnerable in an unsteady job, might feel as though the rug has been pulled from under him when someone close to him dies. A teenager who feels that his parents or his friends don't understand him may look on a death in the family as just another disaster that he has to face. Overwhelmed and particularly vulnerable, this child will need extra support.

## THE SPECIAL NEEDS OF CHILDREN

Even when children seem to be handling a death well—"Just like an adult," as people often put it—they may be confused, filled with fears they find it difficult to express. They need that extra bit of support, attention, and understanding that we don't tend to give to other adults.

I remember one poignant scene. A twelve-year-old boy whose father had died stood by the casket with his mother, greeting the guests. Dressed in a suit and tie, he looked responsible, stable, the man of the family now. His body language said it all, however: stooped over, as though he were carrying the weight of the world on his shoulders; a blank expression, as though someone had turned out the light inside him; a face filled with pain. Life had dealt him a really rotten blow and he was handling it, but inside that façade was a little boy who was desperately afraid. He had not yet been able to start his grieving process.

Take a look at your child's face. Are the muscles tight? Does he seem to be in a state of tension, hostile and hard to talk to? Then maybe he's running away from the issue. On the other hand, it could be that he doesn't really understand the finality of death, which, as I've pointed out, is often the case with a young child. "What's the big deal? Why is everyone so upset?" he or she might think. "Grandpa will only be dead for a little while." An adult who is mourning someone dear to the family can find it unnerving when he thinks that his child doesn't really care that the person died. What he has to realize, when the child is crying bitterly one moment then laughing and jumping around the next, is that the child has also been mourning Grandpa, but he can only handle so much grief. He needs to switch to a different activity at a certain point. We adults often have to do this too, when we're confronted with too much pain—we watch TV, go on a walk, talk on the telephone.

Peter, a teenager I know, played in a tennis match the morning after his father died. In another family, the mother might have found that hard to take. But Peter's mother knew what to expect. She had already sat down with Peter and together they had decided that although Peter was very sad, he would go ahead with the match, that his father would probably have wanted him to play. Peter's mother realized that she couldn't expect a child to grieve as an adult would.

Sometimes in a crisis we adults confuse our own reactions to a death with our child's, projecting on the young person what we're feeling ourselves. John's father had just died and he was deeply disturbed, angry, and feeling guilty because he hadn't spent more time with him. He was generally just miserable. One day it came to a head. "Why are you always so depressed?" he lashed out at his teenage daughter. "Moping around, in a lousy mood. Try to cheer up!" The astonished girl hadn't been feeling blue at all. She wasn't the one who was upset; her father was, and since he couldn't admit his feelings to himself, he projected them onto her. A person who isn't able to come to grips with his own feelings can cause double trouble in the family, putting everyone more on edge than they had been when the death first occurred. Children can do this as well as adults. Being aware of this possibility and talking about it can help prevent a lot of pain.

Very often a child may not seem to be a bit upset about the death of a person he was very close to; he may act as though nothing has happened. It could be that he is avoiding the issue. Maybe he's been getting mixed messages from his parents and feels confused; or maybe he's not ready to deal with it, just as we adults sometimes steer away from unpleasant things we want to avoid.

Four-year-old Sandy was very confused. His mother was crying all the time and when he asked why, she said she had a stomachache. Later, after we had talked about the problem, the mother told Sandy that it was because Grandpa had died and that she was very, very sad because she wouldn't be seeing Grandpa again. Sandy replied, "Don't tell me that story anymore."

That was not an uncommon reply for a child to make. Sandy had had enough. He was confused for the moment, and children tend to shut out things they can't handle. A week or so later, Sandy came back with his questions—he was able to deal with his feelings by then.

Perhaps your child's reaction is concern and regret about the death, but not upset. Some people, children included, are just not that emotional.

> Sean, age fifteen, is a very mature, philosophical kind of young man who has always been thought to be much older than his years. While many of his friends experience great highs and lows, Sean goes through life on an even keel. "When my grandfather died," he explained, "sure, I was sad. For a moment I felt a little rattled, but then I went into a different mode. I felt that that's the way things are—people

have to die someday. I didn't feel guilty or angry; he knew how much I cared for him. And as things in the family became crazier, I got calmer and cooler. The way I looked at it was that my function was to help the rest of the family. There was no question of my feeling like breaking down. I haven't felt like crying in years. That's just not my way of expressing it." Sean added that if it had been his father who died, he might have reacted differently. "My life wasn't as intimately intertwined with Grandpa's as it is with my dad's."

Sean had found his own style of grieving. It was not highly emotional, but neither was it an avoidance of the problem. He talked quietly about his grandfather and told stories about things they had done together, remembering him fondly. Sean didn't need a lot of help to handle the crisis of death, but many youngsters his age do need that extra help.

## THE GRIEVING PROCESS

Each person needs to discover his or her own way of grieving. Trying to stop one child's process by saying something like "Be brave, be a man!" minimizes the significance of the loss and puts an unbelievable burden on that child. To work out their feelings, most children need someone to talk to. Just as the warmth of the sun heals the body, sharing what he feels with someone who cares helps the child heal. For many, tears are therapeutic—a tribute of love for someone who was very dear to them. Others, as I've pointed out, may never shed any tears. If we don't put demands or limitations on our children, by trying to change their grieving process or pretending that it's not going on, the child will grow with the experience.

If you try to cut short the child's grieving process, it may just cause a delayed reaction. In one study on grieving, a story was told about a teenager who had lost both her parents and her boyfriend in a fire. She was left to take care of her younger brothers and sisters. At first she showed cheerful acceptance, then after about two months the impact of the deaths finally hit her. Her responsibilities and the need to maintain the morale of her brothers and sisters had delayed her grieving process. In another really bizarre case, an obviously successful, well-dressed man came to my funeral home once a year on the anniversary of the death of his father, looking for him. Finally, a couple of years ago, he stopped coming, having resolved his grief in some way.

The sudden realization—the breaking of dammed-up feelings—can come at any time, and be triggered by the most innocuous things. Twelve-year-old Bridget was walking down the aisle of the grocery store when all of a sudden tears started streaming down her face. She had seen a box of Instant Ralston, her father's favorite kind of cereal, and it had triggered the release valve for her feelings.

When something like that happens, the time to deal with what that child is feeling is right then—as soon as possible. Don't put it off until a later, more convenient time. Bridget's mother for example, put her arms around her daughter and let her cry for a minute or two; then the child felt better and they went on with their shopping.

### Three Stages of Grief

Dr. John Bowlby of the Tavistock Clinic in London, working with bereaved children, has observed that there are three stages of grief that most children go through—protest, pain, and, finally, hope.

• In the protest stage, the youngster can't believe that the person is dead and tries to get him or her back. One five-year-old I know enlisted the help of a playmate and went to work in her backyard one afternoon, digging up about $300 worth of sod. "I'm looking for Grandpa," she explained to her mother, who came upon the scene about an hour too late. "I miss him. I want him to come home." The little girl, who had been told that Grandpa had died and was buried (although she didn't know anything about where he was buried), figured she'd undo the deed.

The child who faces the death of someone he's loved needs to turn his energies into himself, to talk about how he misses that person. By bringing all the memories to the conscious surface, bit by bit, the child will gradually come to terms with the loss, realizing that the person is dead but never forgotten. The child may need to talk a lot about the dead person, describing in detail all his qualities, how tragic it is that his life was cut short, and how important he was to the youngster. With time, he'll be able to put the memory of the deceased into perspective and move on.

"If you want to heal folks, learn to lay ears on them," writes Doug Manning of Hereford, Texas, in his book *A Minister Speaks About Funerals.* Manning says that by just sitting there listening and not saying much, we can do a tremendous amount of good. He reminds us that people have to solve their own problems; we can't work out someone else's thinking or his feelings. What we can do is stimulate a person to work them out for himself while he talks out what's on his mind. But, cautions Manning, listening is hard to do. "We feel we must say something. To not have an answer is to somehow prove we are not competent. . . . One of the startling discoveries of my life was when I noticed how trained I was to talk and how untrained I was to listen."

The trouble with memories, as Dennis Klass and Audrey Gordon point out in *They Need to Know*, is that before we share them, before we get the feelings out, we act and feel as if the events were in the present when they are actually in the past. By sharing the memories and resolving the feelings, "the present can get some control over the past," and reality takes the place of fantasy.

> Kathy had an abusive father. For years she had hoped he'd die or that her parents would get a divorce; anything to get her father out of her life. One night he got drunk, was hit by a car, and died. "I'm glad he's dead," she admitted sometime later. "I had wished he would die for a long time and now I'm relieved. That's a terrible way to feel. . . . I know I didn't cause him to die but I still feel guilty that I wished so hard."

Once a feeling is expressed, no matter how negative, it doesn't have the power that it did when it was formless. When feelings are put on the table, talked out and looked at in a realistic perspective, they often lose their impact.

As we listen to our children, remember that it's important to make sure that we hear what they're actually saying, not what we *think* they should be saying. We might expect our child to feel lonely or sad, but what comes out of him is that he's relieved or feeling guilty that the person died. His feelings may be very different from what we ourselves are feeling. The temptation is to try and change him. "You shouldn't feel guilty. You did everything you could to help him stay alive"; or, "Even though he treated you badly, he was your father, so you shouldn't feel relieved that he died."

Telling a child he shouldn't feel a certain way, judging his feelings, is an automatic turn-off. Don't judge him, just listen. He has a right to his feelings. They're part of him and he needs to work them out. What he needs to know is that he is not alone; that you're there to help him; that you accept the way he is, bad feelings and all; and that you're trying to empathize. Maybe you've felt that way, too—if so, you can understand what's happening inside him right now. Reassure him that it's okay, it's normal to have these emotions, and that eventually the pain will pass.

• Once reality sets in and the child realizes that the person is gone forever, he may be overwhelmed with pain—feelings of anger and guilt, loneliness, and depression. I'll talk more about these feelings in the pages ahead.

• Eventually, the child realizes that no matter how much he loved the person who died, he can continue life without him, and so he begins to reorganize his life. Despair slowly gives way to hope. It is during this time—after the pain has eased up, when the good days outnumber the bad—that the child will get involved again in things and see options for the future. It may happen at a very definite moment. In one case, the moment of letting go came when a girl helped her mother clean out her father's desk; another child gave away his father's fishing rod in a symbolic gesture of good-bye. But it takes time before a child can make that independent move.

It's important to remember that all of the feelings associated with grief ebb and flow, and that you and your child will inevitably go back over these emotions time and again. We love to neatly compartmentalize things, to finish with one, then go on to the next. But it doesn't work that way with the emotions of grief.

Like Sean, the fifteen-year-old I talked about earlier, your child might not go through many of the emotions. Gwen Schwartz-Borden, a social worker who does bereavement counseling on Long Island, New York, remembered one woman who came to her after reading a book on dealing with grief. Very upset, she asked, "Am I going to go crazy like this book says? I've never been a person who acted crazy!" The woman thought that there must be some recipe for grief, and because she didn't feel crazy she wasn't following directions; she wasn't doing it right!

How long does the grieving process take? According to the late Dr. Erich Lindeman, that depends on how well the person does the "grief work." During this process, a person frees himself from his bond to the dead person, readjusts his life, and forms new relationships. It may go more quickly for some than for others. Dr. Hal Fishkin compares the process to a sore that needs to heal. "If you have a wound, you clean it and expose it to fresh air and the light of day. Then you take away all the damaged tissue and make it as clean as possible so that normal healing can take place . . . and that takes time." He adds that after six months the child who has lost someone very close to him probably won't be as depressed as he was after two weeks, but that it's difficult to generalize. "Different children need different things. Some have such a turbulent emotional response that they need much more help."

Some people who aren't able to work out their grief never resolve it; they may learn to live with their pain, but it never leaves. Most youngsters are able to bounce back with resiliency; remember, though, that grief is an emotion that recurs sporadically. Almost anything can trigger the pain—a song, the smell of a certain flower; an anniversary or holiday, even as much as a year later, can be the worst time. Gwen Schwartz-Borden notes that just when you think you're better, the pain can start up again. "Just when reality sets in and the numbness wears off, months after the death, it may all of a sudden hit the child again . . . all that yearning and searching for the dead person. It's like a woman with false labor pains."

## PROBLEMS TO BE PREPARED FOR AT VARIOUS AGES

Much of what we've covered so far in this chapter has been how older children react to a death. They're the ones who usually have a tougher time and take longer to work through their pain and anxiety. With little children, we have to spend more time finding out what they think, clearing up misconceptions, and helping them understand that the person is really dead forever. Young children also experience pain—it may not last as long as that of an older child, but it is still often very severe.

In Chapter 1, we took a look at what children in each major age group might think and understand about death. The children in each of these groups also have predictable reactions when confronted with the death of someone close to them.

### Age Two to Six

Little children will probably be clingy, afraid to let you go out, concerned that they'll lose you, too. Over and over again they might ask, "Hasn't he been dead enough?" Don't get frustrated. Death is a hard concept for little ones to understand, and eventually it'll sink in. With fewer resources to help them deal with their feelings, they still have to go through the same stages of grief that an adult or older child does. To make things more complicated, their minds are also filled with magical thinking. According to Gwen Schwartz-Borden, that magical thinking and the "I did it" syndrome are the most common problems bereaved children have—waiting for the dead person to come back, or thinking that they caused the death of the person.

The very young child usually doesn't know that he's grieving, he just knows that he feels bad—and since he usually doesn't have the vocabulary or the experience to explain what he's feeling, he speaks to us in symbolic language, acting out his feelings in fantasy play.

> Bill, John, and Mary Ellen were very close to Grandpa. He lived on the next block in the city, just a two-minute bicycle ride around the corner, and each summer they all went to the country together. During the first summer after Grandpa died the children seldom talked about him, but he was still a part of their lives. They played in the backyard, watching the chipmunk (which Grandpa had confided told him secrets!), and pulling the weeds out of the garden that the old man had tended so carefully. Finally one afternoon they locked themselves in their room, and, taking all the clothes out of the dresser drawer, they lined it with a blanket. Next, they put candles on top of the bureau and opened a prayer book to prayers for the dead. Bill and John then dressed up in sheets so they'd look like priests and they put Mary Ellen in the dresser drawer, their make-believe coffin. She lay there quietly while Bill and John sang their funeral songs. All three children participated in their make-believe funeral, saying good-bye to Grandpa. Years later, the three

of them still talk about that afternoon with fondness. Theirs was a family where the children felt free to grieve in the way they chose.

Remember that when we try to explain something, we use our minds to form the ideas into words, very often pushing away the feelings. Since children don't have the command of the language that we do or the experience to express how they feel, they often relate nonverbally, on an emotional level, understanding a look in your eyes or the gentle tone of your voice just as much as the words you're saying. Allow your child to be open and express how he feels. Then he'll be comfortable enough to come back for more information. Children adjust more quickly when they feel that they're in on things, and that their parents understand how they're feeling. By talking with your child in an open, direct manner, by holding his hand and letting him cry, you say, "I understand, I'm with you."

Sharing your feelings with a young child on a level he'll understand can help him realize that his own feelings are okay. Here's what you might say to a three- or four-year-old: "I feel very, very sad that Grandpa died, and very, very mad because Grandpa didn't take good care of himself and he didn't take his medicine like he was supposed to. I wanted him to live. We'll all be lonesome for Grandpa and we'll miss him a lot and sometimes we'll be crying." More information can be added, depending on the age and maturity of the child.

One researcher in the field of child bereavement described the way a little boy whose brother had died handled his grief in his fantasy play: he buried his brother's toys in the sandbox. Gradually, the child worked through his grief:

his parents put a picture of the dead child in the boy's room; the family started to talk about how they missed his brother; and finally, one by one, the child removed the toys from the sandbox and put them back on the shelf.

Jenny's mother was similarly sensitive to her child's reactions. After her mother had explained the facts, four-year-old Jenny asked when she could see Grandpa again. Her mother explained, "Not for a long, long time, after you die and get buried and go to heaven." But Jenny, like many children her age, was persistent. "Will God make him better and send him back?" "No," answered the mother. "Once a person's body stops working, it won't work anymore, and he is dead. He won't come back." The mother said Jenny accepted that pretty well, after she had cried for a while. "Then I said, 'No matter what happens, you still have me.' And she's seemed fine ever since."

## Age Six to Nine

Very often, children in this age group may be preoccupied with morbid thoughts, fascinated by the image of death stalking around, scared of the bogeyman. Louise was that age, in the early days of grammar school, when the reclusive old lady next door to her died. The word got around that the old lady's house was haunted, and that her ghost snatched children who walked by at night. The street was off limits for months, with the children in the neighborhood taking great precautions to avoid that block on their way to school. Louise, by association, was singled out. After all, she had been the lady's next-door neighbor, and she was a rather shy girl, so she was labeled weird and creepy; she didn't have one friend; the children avoided her. Not able to understand why they feel afraid or confused, children at this age some-times try to find a scapegoat to embody their fears.

If they're embarrassed or don't know how to behave, they may act silly or laugh; on the other hand, they may become suddenly quiet when they see a person who in their mind is associated with death. Stevie, a nine-year-old whose father had just died, noticed that the other kids wouldn't "goof off" if he was around. Maybe they felt that when someone dies everyone should always act serious. But for Stevie, so re-cently traumatized by his father's death, the reaction of his classmates made this time even harder. Suddenly, he was not only alone in his grief, he was an outsider. Children need to be told what to say and how to act when someone dies. Most of them are probably not aware of how they may be hurting other children.

At this age, children coping with a death may be feeling guilty or angry, or may be afraid that their parents will die. They often show their concern with questions such as, "How old are you?" (meaning, "Are you going to die too?"), or with increased interest in a parent's health. Explaining away his fears will help him feel better:

> "Remember how cranky Grandpa was the last few times we saw him? Well, that's because he was so sick. Some chil-dren might think that they did something that caused a per-son to die—that maybe because they talked back to him or made too much noise and got him upset, that's why he died. But those things just don't make people die."

As with the younger children, playing often helps older ones to work out their stressful situations. It is through play, say the experts, that a child can achieve mastery over a situ-ation he doesn't understand and work through his anxiety.

Some children paint sad pictures; others might play violent games in which cars crash and burn to get their feelings out. Encourage your child to talk about the dead person, to relive the good times and the bad. Unlike the younger child, who probably remembers just the surface aspects (what he looked like, the fact that he had curly hair), the "middle" child remembers more enduring qualities—the fact that Grandma used to go on walks with her and tell her stories; the fact that she was kind and funny. And it's those qualities this child will probably miss. "He won't be sitting at his favorite place in the bleachers watching me play ball anymore." "Who will go blueberry-picking with me now?"

When there's a death close to home, the world may seem to be tumbling down. Eight-year-old Kevin's mother died. Right at the same time a tropical plant that the family had brought back from a vacation, nurturing it and growing from a seedling, wilted and died. Then, on the day of the funeral, Kevin and his father walked into their house and found their pet bird lying dead in its cage. The child was very upset. "What is it about us that makes everything die?" Kevin's father had to help him understand that these events were completely unrelated ("We were visiting Mom at the hospital so much I forgot to water the plants," etc.).

## Age Nine to Twelve

Trying to be grownup, the preteen is still at least some of the time in the world of fantasy. He or she probably grasps death intellectually but may be having a hard time letting it sink in. Children this age do not want to seem different from the other kids. "How should I act?" "What do I say to Grandma?" They can also be very judgmental about themselves and everyone around them. "I really looked so stupid crying. I shouldn't have been so upset. I knew she was sick. . . ." "Aunt Molly really put on a scene. Was I embarrassed!" "Grandpa looked really gross! Lying there in the casket he looked really phoney!"

Becoming very much their own people, children this age may be critical or sensitive, catty or kind. Bridget, the preteen we met earlier in the aisles of the supermarket, used to come into her mother's room and sit quietly holding her hand when she knew her mother was crying . . . not saying a word, just being there to let her mother know she cared. Bryan, another sensitive child, feeling irritable and confused, didn't want to bother other people with his grief—so he isolated himself in his room every night, afraid he might antagonize his friends. Each thing that he tried seemed to take an enormous amount of effort and it made him frustrated, short-tempered. After a month or so he had worked things through, and he started coming out of his room and getting involved in things again. "Boy, I guess I never realized how, important Grandpa was to me," he finally said.

### Teenagers

By the time a child is in his teens, he will probably have many of the same feelings and reactions to a death that an adult would. But the way he processes his grief—his behavior—may be very different. A wildly hysterical outburst may be followed immediately by embarrassed laughter as the child tries to get a grip on himself, to act like an adult. One moment he may idealize the dead person, making him superhuman, the next moment condemn him. His emotions may be in an uproar and he doesn't know how to help himself.

Teenagers are very concerned with their image and what

the other kids think of them, and sometimes when they are actually raging against the world they appear to be strong, stoic, and cool. They often hate having people see them cry. Because of this, their emotions may erupt in physical distress—changes in the nervous or hormonal system, headaches, hyperventilation, or hyperactivity. A girl's menstrual period may stop for a few months. Another child may act indifferent, expressing helplessness by pretending the death didn't happen. Still another may criticize what's happening around him, or philosophize about how futile life is. In the crisis of death, a teenager's whole system of belief may be thrown topsy-turvy, and a child who's disturbed may start acting very much out of character; in extreme situations, trying to forget through overeating, alcohol, or drugs. Very often at the base of that compulsive behavior are two of the common elements of grief—anger and guilt.

## DEALING WITH ANGER, GUILT, AND RESPONSIBILITY

The backyard looked like a monsoon had struck it— swamped with water, some of the puddles two inches deep. It was a day to sit inside and read a book or watch television, but eleven-year-old Ted wanted to go camping. He had taken his tent out of his closet and was starting to ready all his gear when his father happened to walk by his room. "What are you up to?" the father asked. "I'm going to pitch my tent in the backyard," Ted answered. "You can't do that! It's pouring out there!" "I'm going to do it anyhow," Ted said angrily.

Several days before, Ted's uncle had died and the emotions had been building steadily inside him. He was ready to burst. He didn't know what to do, but he had to do something, so he decided to put up his tent. When his father questioned this, he lashed out; fortunately, his father understood what was happening, and after they sat down together and talked it all out, the gear went back in the closet.

People get angry because, like Ted, they feel out of control, impotent, helpless. Anger is an emotion that's hard to express openly, because showing it is generally not acceptable in our society. If you don't express it in some way, though, it's hard to shake. It may burst out in all sorts of ways — shouting at friends, snide remarks to a teacher, a hostile reaction when a parent asks a question.

When a person dies, there are plenty of things to be angry about. Your child might be angry at the doctor for not being able to cure the person, at God for not making him better, at you for not making the person who died take his medicine, even at the person who died for self-destructive behavior or abandoning the family. This anger may be justified. You can imagine the rage a child would feel at the drunken driver who killed his mother! In other circumstances, the anger may be misplaced.

One man told me that once he was just about to throw another guy through the window of a restaurant for a nasty remark when he suddenly stopped in mid-fight and realized what he was doing. "At the moment, I remembered that you had said I might be angry with my father for dying. At the time I thought to myself, 'Oh, I wouldn't do that.' Well, here I was, about ready to kill this guy, and I suddenly realized why I was so mad."

Anger is an emotion I see frequently as a funeral director. I see people frustrated at not being able to help the one that they loved survive, and so they lash out at those closest to them. Very often, kids pick up the anger of their parents, and what may look like arrogant, hostile misbehavior coming from youngsters may be suppressed anger. Each child will find his own way of ventilating that anger, satisfying the loss of control that he feels. Emily, a seven-year-old, chose the funeral home as the setting for bringing her anger to a head.

> Everyone in the family came to Grandpa's wake and Emily was even given a new dress for the occasion — a pretty light-blue smocked frock with lace. The family all went into the viewing room, gathering with the other relatives, talking and hugging each other. Even Emily's ten-year-old brother, George, was allowed in. But not Emily. She had to sit outside in the hall, and wait till the others came out. Looking back, Emily still remembers how angry she was to be left out like that. "I was so mad I wouldn't even talk about Grandpa. And I never wore that dress again. I absolutely refused. I wanted to let the family know how angry I was . . . that they should have let me come in with them. He was my grandpa and I wanted to say good-bye."

Occasionally, younger children may be more in touch with their feelings than older ones, whose minds have become muddled with all kinds of emotions. Bereavement counselor Gwen Schwartz-Borden tells the story of a five-year-old who told her that sometimes he gets really mad because his father died. And when he does, he beats up his brother. I'm glad I'm not that brother! But at least the mother knows what's happening when the boys get in a brawl. If the anger surfaces in the family, the moment may not be a pleasant one, but the parent gets a chance to see it firsthand and take steps to deal with it.

One way to deal with this anger is to encourage the child to express how angry he is, help him find some kind of outlet. Dan, a writer I know, told his daughter Maya that whenever he gets angry and frustrated, he goes out into the backyard with a tennis racket and beats the daylights out of a certain bush. Horticultural enthusiasts may not be very happy about this solution, but for this man it works. Maya decided her pillow was a better object of aggression and she spent a lot of time cleaning feathers out of her room. One father bought his son a punching bag to help him work out his anger at the loss of his younger brother; some people listen to music, others chop wood, go running, or scrub floors. Whatever releases the pent-up anger—as long as it doesn't hurt anyone—is fine.

But talking it all out is really the key to helping a child through the anger. If you feel angry too, you might say something like, "I'm really angry at Daddy for dying, and it makes me feel terrible that I feel that way because I know that he didn't want to die—but just the same, I do feel that way. And feelings are something that we can't control. We can control the way we act because of those feelings, but we can't control the feelings."

Anger is an emotion that is directed out at something; guilt is an emotion that is directed inward, often as a result of anger. The two go hand in hand when there's a death, and when they're allowed to fester they cause both adults and children a lot of grief.

"He shouldn't have gotten drunk that night." (Anger) "If only I had taken the keys away." (Guilt) "He shouldn't have run himself into the ground working so hard." (Anger) "If only I had realized what he was doing and tried to stop him, maybe he wouldn't have had the heart attack." (Guilt)

Children need the support of their parents or someone close to help them deal with these feelings and overcome the "I did it" syndrome. Caught in a vicious cycle of emotions, fifteen-year-old Kelly got angry at her father for dying, then felt guilty because of it, then angry again because she felt guilty. She felt she was losing her mind. Carol was just ten when her sister died after an illness of several months, during which her mother had to be at the hospital. "And all that time, I wished my sister would die because I wanted my mother back. When she did die, I felt relieved, but guilty, too." A couple of years later, her mother died. Emily, feeling that her wishful thinking had killed her sister, figured she was being punished with her mother's death. With no one to talk to about all this, she bottled up the feelings until she nearly burst.

Children, like adults, sometimes scourge themselves psychologically for not preventing the inevitable. "If only I hadn't put the stuffed animal in his crib last night" . . . "If only I hadn't gone to the store just at that moment." This guilt is irrational, as in the case of an eleven-year-old girl who blamed herself for never mailing a "get well" card to her aunt. "It was in my pocketbook, but I never took it to the mailbox," she kept repeating to her mother. The mother was amazed. "It's as though she thinks the card would have saved my sister's life."

Sometimes the guilt has a basis in fact. One teenaged girl was taking forever to brush her teeth, trying to push her father's patience to the limit. After about fifteen minutes, the father said to the child, "Come on now, you're making me sick!" and he clutched his chest. Within the hour, he was dead of a heart attack.

That unfortunate child did have something to do with her father's death and she required therapy to help work it through, but she wasn't the sole cause; she was just one of the final triggers. The man's heart was ready for an attack. The death had a biological cause.

Since guilt is often related to the cause of death, make sure your child has a good grasp of what happened to the dead person. Make him realize that there was something biologically wrong, so he won't be haunted for years by the thought that he could somehow have prevented it. When a child feels that there's no way to "make up" for a real or imagined wrong, when he has no chance to "do right" by the dead person, it's a terrible burden to carry.

One way to stop this kind of self-recrimination is to tell the children if you know that a person is very sick or dying. Give them a chance to say good-bye and say, "I'm sorry," to start working through whatever guilt they may have and deal with their grief. As Leo Lefebvre, a bereavement counselor in Delaware, points out, grief is a process we have to go through, and we grow according to how well we experience this process. There's no healthy way around it, only through it.

## HELPING YOUR CHILD TO HEAL

Each person has their own coping mechanism for dealing with pain; sometimes it's religious, sometimes it's a physical aid. Gordon and Klass in *They Need to Know* describe one grieving technique for getting rid of unfinished business, those feelings of guilt, anger, and loss. They suggest that you and your child find a quiet place and sit down with a picture of the dead person; then, talking to the picture, get your child to express all the positive and negative feelings that are in his or her heart. "You may feel silly at first," they say, "but some people have found it helpful in saying good-bye."

Maybe there's a book or prayer that you turn to when you're upset, or perhaps a comforting idea. Share these with your child. Dorothy told her grandchildren that when the world crashes in and she thinks she just can't handle things anymore, her trick is to "Golden Key the condition." In her mind, there's a big box that she puts troubles in . . . troubles that are beyond the grasp of everyday living. "And when things get to be too much, I just put the trouble in the box in my mind, lock it up with a golden key, and hand the key over to God."

As he passes through grief into healing, our youngster needs a continuity of care, one person to follow him through the experience—someone he trusts implicitly, someone he feels free to unload his feelings on. If you can't talk with your child (and some people just can't), find someone who can, such as a close friend or relative who will have the necessary patience and understanding.

> Whenever there was a death in the family, Aunt Helen somehow always ended up with the little children. Children know when they can sit on someone's lap and when they can't; who they can confess to when they've been naughty, and who they had better steer clear of. And Aunt Helen was someone they could talk to.
>
> Death, in Aunt Helen's mind, wasn't anything to be feared. On warm spring afternoons she often took the little ones bike-riding down the paths of the neighborhood cemetery, pointing out the pretty flowers and where all the relatives were buried. Calm and accepting, Aunt Helen thought of death as a part of life. So, every time there was a wake in the family, Aunt Helen was the one who took care of the kids. She never got ruffled; the children felt comfortable with her and she with them.

As I've noted, how children react and how they heal are often affected by how the adults around them react. Sometimes a bereaved child who comes from a calm environment and is not used to seeing emotion overtly displayed can be threatened by open affection. Having relatives he hardly knows hugging and kissing him may scare him, and he may retreat into a shell. To open him up, to regain his trust, try to quiet his world. Calmly help him talk about what's on his mind.

For some children, the upheaval of their family by the death of a parent or sibling may be aggravated by another major change, such as a move to another city. If it's at all possible, when there's a death in the family, try not to make another big change in routine right away. We may not be able to control the way we feel, but we can control how those feelings are expressed, how we make decisions, and how we handle ourselves and our lives. "I see this is a family thing," says bereavement counselor Gwen Schwartz-Borden. "When there's a death, I don't single the kids out and just counsel them on how to deal with it. It's a problem the whole family has to face."

## Others May Disagree with Your Approach

As with many parenting issues, the decision to talk with your children openly about death may be criticized by well-meaning friends and relatives who don't believe in the kind of openness we've been talking about. "What do you mean, you're bringing him to the funeral? In our family we just don't do things like that!" "He's going to a movie on the day before his mother's funeral? I've never heard of such a thing!" "Did you see Jamie? He wasn't even wearing a suit and tie!"

My advice is based on a relationship between parent and child in which the parent sees the child as a person with a right to know what's happening around him, a right to get help in this time of crisis, and a right to express how he's feeling in his own way. Along with all these rights, the child also has a responsibility to do what he can to help the team, as it were—the family. But some people will resist your way of doing things or even oppose your efforts, either with an all-out onslaught or subtle skirmishes.

I recall when Mimi sat in my office with her two elderly aunts, going over the details of her father's funeral. When I asked her what she planned to say to her five-year-old, the two aunts broke in. "Oh, he doesn't know a thing! No need to tell him or bother him about all this." "Oh, yes, he needs to know!" Mimi asserted, and then we talked about what she would say to the child about his grandfather's death. All through our conversation, the two aunts muttered to each other about how ridiculous this all was. "Why upset the child?" Finally, Mimi stopped and glared at them. "He's going to be told and he's going to be part of the funeral!" she said.

Another family came in to see me with a thirteen-year-old. Brad was with his mother, father, grandmother, and Uncle Tom, who kept grumbling about how this kid should not be here. Finally, the whole group got up to go look at a casket, and Uncle Tom stopped Brad. "You can't come," he said. The child's reply: "Why not? I'm going to see it anyhow later on; why not now?" The boy went with his parents to help pick out the casket, with the uncle grudgingly going along.

Brad's uncle thought he was doing the right thing; so did Mimi's two aunts. Most relatives offering advice mean well, but they are not the child's parents. Only you as parents know what you want to say to your children, and in what kind of atmosphere you want to raise them.

One mother whose husband had died was advised by a dear friend, a rabbi, not to say anything to her five-year-old about his father's death. "He won't even remember his father three months from now." How do you respond to advice like that? I suggest that you explain where your values are on this. Say something like, "Listen, this is something that I believe is really important to this child and I must do it. I have to tell him the truth and let him be part of this funeral. Now, I'd really like your support. I'd love to have you help me out and I'll tell you what I'm saying to him. But please don't try to change it. "

Finally, remember that most of these people will be with you for just a few days. You are the one who has to live with your child's questions.

### Let Your Child Know
### What to Expect from Others

It's comforting to a child to know how different people in the family group will act when they're grieving. Take a good look at the family and describe to your child what he'll be seeing. "Aunt Sadie will probably get hysterical when she sees Grandpa. Uncle Ned will probably sit in the corner quietly and not talk with anyone." Also, prepare him for what people may say, so when he gets mixed messages he knows how to handle them. "Uncle Jim may tell you to be strong because men don't cry, but you'll see other men crying because that's what some people do when they feel sad."

Some people don't know how to talk to children as if they were people. The only way they can communicate is by telling fairy tales that blur the distinction in the youngster's mind between fact and fancy.

Tell your child that sometimes people feel so bad because a person died that they get a little confused. They think that not telling children what really happened—that telling a make-believe story—will make the children feel better and not miss the person who died. One mother I know told her five-year-old that this would happen. At the wake, her child came up to her. "Mommy, Uncle Bill just told me that Grandma is asleep and she'll be getting up later. He did that because he doesn't want me to feel bad, right?"

If the foundation is laid, your child will be better able to accept the negative aspects of the family support system. When Sean, the cool-headed teenager we met earlier in this chapter, was asked by a distraught aunt why he didn't seem very upset that Grandpa had died, he knew how to deal with the question. "I knew she was under a lot of stress so I didn't worry about it. I figured that's just the way she is."

## Give Your Child the Opportunity to Participate and Help

Judy's husband died of cancer slowly, over the course of a year and a half. During that time, Dawn, their ten- year-old daughter, knew what was going on, helped out where she could, and grieved with her parents as her father died. There were no secrets. When the end finally came, Dawn was prepared. She was upset, but she had said her good- byes, helped her father in his last days, and was able to han- dle her loss rather well.

The key to this kind of open communication, where a child is free to say what's on his mind and where he feels se- cure within his family, is a place for him within the support network. Let him be an active part of the group. Young children can answer the doorbell or go on errands; older children can help make funeral arrangements, answer the phone, or pick people up at the airport. Ask your child what he wants to do to help, and make sure he knows that you *need* that help. By being part of the system, he'll learn a lot—seeing how other people handle themselves, how they grieve. It will show him that he is able to handle difficult emotions and to help other people.

# 4

## Expectations for the Grieving Child and the Best Ways to Respond

It is extremely important to respond appropriately when coming in contact with anyone who is grieving or suffering from trauma, and this is particularly evident with a child. How you react in these situations can help create a more comfortable, supportive atmosphere, particularly if you are prepared and have an idea what to expect.

In many ways, setting up the proper kind of environment to help the child is the most critical factor. The crucial question then becomes: How best to create a supportive atmosphere that allows the child to go through the process of grieving, which must take its own time and due course. We realize, early on, that healing from grief may be a long process. There seems to be no way to rush it, and it often appears that there is so little we can actually do, much to our consternation. "It's frustrating," said a father, "not to be able to take away my child's pain."

What added to this father's frustration was the fact that he was grieving the same loss as his son.

You can best assist the child by establishing the optimal support system through choosing from the best-equipped, available caregivers. This requires realistically evaluating your existing support system, which might include the primary caregivers as well as siblings, grandparents, other relatives, teachers, school counselors, athletic coaches, camp counselors, and any other responsible, caring person. All of these caregivers can make a tremendous difference if they are well-informed about the particular circumstances and apprised of what kind of behavior they might expect. Too often some of these valuable potential helpers are overlooked, and it is extremely worthwhile to call in all the help that you feel comfortable with because the grieving person can only benefit from an extended supportive environment.

Many of us who have experienced a loss can recall statements made in passing that plainly showed there was no comprehension of what we were going through. Therefore, whether as a parent, grandparent, sibling, or teacher of the child, we must be informed about what to expect from the grieving child, and also learn how to respond to certain situations. What we say at what particular time may have a great impact.

Responses to attempts to care for children and adults alike who have experienced loss seem to be made up of extremes: Either your efforts make things better or they make them worse. Most often the results depend not on what you do but on how you respond with what you know. Many caregivers are surprised to discover that "just being there" may be more important than what you say or do.

The following sections describe a child's normal responses to a loss. Of course, crisis situations, such as the shootings at Columbine High School in Colorado or the bombing in Oklahoma City, or the devastation of the hijacked planes crashing into the World Trade Towers and the Pentagon, or any other sudden traumatic incident, present additional challenges that will be discussed in further detail below in the section on trauma.

## WHAT YOU NEED TO KNOW ABOUT GRIEF

Therese Rando, in her book *Treatment for Complicated Mourning*, points out the importance of understanding certain myths about mourning and the pressure that these myths can place on those coping with loss. Some of the deeply embedded myths she describes include:

- Grief and mourning decline steadily over time.
- All losses prompt the same type of mourning.
- Bereaved individuals need only express feelings to resolve loss.
- Health involves putting the deceased out of their mind.
- Bereaved individuals will only be affected psychologically.
- Intensity and length of mourning are testimony to love of the deceased.
- One grieves only the loss of the individual and nothing else.
- Sudden, unexpected death is the same as one that is anticipated.
- Mourning is over after a year.

The grieving process may take longer than expected. Since no two people grieve exactly in the same way, traditional beliefs about what should constitute "proper" grieving often distort the reality of the grieving process. When these old-fashioned notions are used to decide how a child or adult is doing, that person is often misjudged.

It is important to note that grief changes. There are good days and not so good days. Some difficult days can be anticipated, such as anniversaries, traditional holidays, and locations that bring back memories.

There are times that grief takes over when you least expect it. What's important is that you realize that it's normal and okay, and that those around the grieving person realize the same.

Grief requires enormous energy.

Grief involves not only loss of the present but also the future.

Many situations such as accidents where there are only sole survivors produce grief and trauma reactions that are often unrecognized.

In whatever capacity you may interact with a person who is grieving a loss or a victim of a traumatic event, it may be helpful to consider the limitations on personal performance that may be imposed by the normal dynamics of grief. Consider how the following mental traits might affect the grieving individual and whether he or she is aware of these dynamics.

- Short attention span
- Impaired decision-making
- Inability or difficulty concentrating
- Impeded functioning
- Sense of being preoccupied
- Feeling of going crazy
- Tendency to socially withdraw

- Disorganization
- Disorientation
- Being pressured by the agenda of others

There are also physical symptoms to be on the lookout for:

- Sensitivity to stimuli
- Restlessness
- Weight gain or loss
- Bitterness
- Headaches
- Anger or guilt
- Irritability
- Sleeping difficulties
- Heart palpitations
- Blurred vision
- Lacking normal strength and energy

Who might find this information useful:

- Parents certainly, as well as grandparents, must know about the grieving process to best help each other as well as a grieving child. It's interesting that grandparents are often overlooked as a support system when parents are available. There are millions of children who are being raised today, solely or in part by their grandparents. It is important to recognize that parents often have the difficult task of providing support, stability, and reassurance to their children at a time when they may personally be experiencing the impact of their child's exposure to trauma or having been victims themselves. Often they are attempting to help their child when they have the least reserve.

- Siblings often become responsible to offer support to younger children in their family.
- Teachers are on the frontlines of both a child's development, education, and emotional support during a normal grief experience or a traumatic crisis. Barrie Sue Zicherman, an educator and consultant to parent groups, highlights the need to provide teachers and staff with information and resources before a crisis. Teachers' tasks are complicated on a variety of levels. Certainly they must support the student whose experience occurs outside the school environment. But when the crisis occurs within the school, they are confronted with their own reaction as well as their whole class. Viewing the scenario in this manner illustrates the critical need to support the educator emotionally and with every resource possible.
- School psychologists must be able to provide assistance and suggest further resources for children, parents, and teachers alike.
- And, of course, mental health providers, particularly those who specialize in treating trauma and grief, have to be up to date on how to handle grieving children in a sensitive and optimal way.

### The Impact of Grief on Business and Management

Managers or supervisors must be aware of the effect that employee grief and trauma experiences can have on them personally and on workplace issues, such as increased stress, errors, omissions, accidents, safety, customer service, employee relations and productivity, absenteeism, and sick leave.

There are some compelling reasons for companies to look carefully at the impact of trauma and grief in their workplace:

1. Financial. Unrecognized grief fallout can be extremely expensive and emotionally draining, both short and long term. In addition until it is identified, the problems will continue unabated.
2. Staff support. If a company cultivates a caring atmosphere that recognizes loss and maintains a support staff equipped for handling grieving, then this usually brings very positive responses from the workers. With a good support team, a company that has gone through a corporate downsizing, for instance, can help the current employees bond with a shared feeling of survival.
3. Management and supervisor support. Grief can place enormous pressure on the process of goal achievement, and therefore must be addressed in a healthy, supportive, open manner.
4. Enhanced corporate loyalty. A sense of commitment to a company grows stronger in a caring corporate culture.
5. The bottomline: It's the right thing to do.

It was just three weeks after the death of Jack's thirty-two-year-old son that Jack's traffic violations began to pile up. "First it was two speeding tickets back to back," Jack recalls. "A week later I passed a stop sign and shortly after that incident, I ran a red light. Honestly," Jack says, "I don't remember seeing the stop sign or the red light. I was lucky no one was injured." Jack expected to grieve but he was totally un-prepared for his lack of concentration and surprised that a perfect forty-year driving record could fall to the grieving process.

Carol, a young widow, reports driving to work in the early morning hours and finding herself driving on the other side of the double white line. "Luckily, there was no traffic. I couldn't believe that my concentration was so affected. Maybe if I had known what to expect, I could have been more careful."

We usually don't have to look far to find comparable ex-amples in our personal life or in our workplaces. With this in mind we might wonder whether today's managers are sensitized to the impact of personal life transition issues on individuals and on their work environment? Do they have enough knowledge to deal effectively with the loss and its effects?

Managerial effectiveness and success are dependent on an enhanced understanding of human behavior. Sadly, we discover that, for a variety of reasons, there is little, if any, in-formation presented to people who will surely confront the grieving process on a regular basis. What can be expected of a grieving individual or a grieving staff?

In addition to the more common managerial challenges of today's workplace, failure to anticipate and develop strate-gies to respond to these issues surrounding loss routinely re-sult in costly errors, omissions, and accidents.

Productivity, morale, customer relations, and public image all have the potential to be impacted by employee loss experiences. Obvious losses such as separation, divorce, and death along with mergers and downsizing create a con-stellation of reactions that can effect the survivors many months and years after the actual event.

"I should have spoken to you four months ago," Mike began. "My controller's brother died after a long bout with cancer, and my office is in a shambles. Grant proposals are way behind, invoices haven't been sent out. I can't believe the impact that her loss has had on the overall functioning of our office and her co-workers."

"Mike," I said, "we should have begun the day she told you about her brother's illness. That was the beginning. It was where planning for her period of loss and transition could have begun. It was your opportunity to create an environment that was supportive, productive, and nurturing, both as her brother was dying as well as during her grieving process. Now we are playing catch-up."

Mike thought that his assistant would be okay and as productive as usual after a few days off. In addition he believed that his employee assistance program alone would be enough to return his assistant quickly to her pre-loss emotional status.

Looking back, Mike realized that his controller had began to respond to her brother's illness early on and had already started to exhibit the impact of this family tragedy with erratic, unusual behavior.

## TRAUMATIC STRESS

The following information and resources are provided as a guide toward enhanced understanding of the impact of trauma on both children and adults. The intention is not that this material will enable you to treat trauma but rather to recognize the need to identify symptoms and reach out to the increasing number of specialists in the area of trauma.

A person, an adult or a child, who has experienced a traumatic event does not necessarily develop Post-Traumatic

Stress Disorder, or PTSD. Familiarity with symptoms of PTSD are important, however, because familiarity with the symptoms may reduce the possibility that one might overlook a need for professional intervention. PTSD can follow a traumatic death as well as a traumatic event.

- Psychologists consider the death of a loved one to be the single most upsetting, stressful, and feared event in a person's life.
- A sudden or violent death is even more of a shock than one that is expected, such as after a long illness.
- A suicide can be particularly devastating, because family members often blame themselves for not preventing the suicide.
- For most people, intense feelings of grief subside after six months to a year, but some people may experience what is known as "post-traumatic stress," especially when memories of the loss are triggered by an anniversary or other event. About 15 to 25 percent of bereaved individuals show signs of significant distress, particularly major depression, as much as one or two years after losing a loved one. This intense, persistent, extremely distressing response is referred to as "Post-Traumatic Stress Syndrome" (PTSD). Strictly defined, the term refers to the aftermath of an event that posed a threat to the person's life or safety, such as a physical assault, a transportation accident, or military combat. But even events that are not life-threatening, such as the loss of a loved one, can cause a lingering or delayed intense reaction, perhaps surfacing at an unexpected time and seemingly unrelated to the loss.

PTSD would be more likely to afflict a surviving family member if their loved one died as the result of a violent accident or malicious crime. Individuals with PTSD relive their terror and helplessness again and again in their thoughts and dreams, perhaps triggered by changes in brain chemistry resulting from the trauma. To block this psychic pain, they avoid anything associated with the trauma. Left untreated, PTSD can take a severe toll—physically, mentally, and socially.

According to author Therese Rando, traumatic events are characterized by their suddenness, randomness, and lack of anticipation. They are often violent and destructive. They are perceived as being preventable, often involving negligence and carelessness. Sometimes the traumatic event involves multiple deaths without the recovery of the body of the deceased. This further complicates the mourning process, preventing the survivors from taking advantage of the therapeutic benefits of viewing the body along with the traditional funeral rituals.

If the event was intentionally malicious, there is an additional set of dynamics for the survivors.

Accidents, suicide, and homicide may involve posttraumatic stress as well as a sense of victimization. In some cases, such as suicide or criminal circumstances surrounding a death, a social stigma may arise toward the survivors. Trauma may also be inflicted from confronting the death of others as well as from a personal life-threatening experience.

It is important to recognize the following dynamics in people suffering from a traumatic experience. If you have been the victim of a trauma, it's important to notice and accept some of these conditions in yourself.

- A decrease in the capacity to cope
- An extended period of acute grief
- Loss of a feeling of personal security
- A loss of confidence in the world as we know it
- A shattering of our assumptive world because things like this  are not supposed to happen
- The possible emergence of Post-Traumatic Stress Disorder

### Caregiver Comfort Zone in a Trauma Situation

Caregivers fall into a variety of categories, from family, friends, and co-workers to clergy and trained professionals. Sometimes the caregivers' comfort zone depends on how close they are emotionally to the grieving or traumatized person. Trauma centers with specially trained medical and support personnel are designed to respond to a myriad of sudden, life-threatening events in a professional way.

It's always difficult to be in the presence of behavior that is unexpected or that seems abnormal. Responses to both grief and trauma, although different, are normal responses to abnormal situations. Fred Nenner, director of social work for the trauma center at Lutheran Medical Center in Brooklyn, New York, knows how important and difficult it is, even for trained professionals, to be " in that space" with the family of a trauma victim, without feeling that the situation must be fixed.

Nenner, in his story "Nellie," describes the members of the Level 1 Trauma Team as "all exquisitely prepared through years of training for their special part to keep people alive when terrible things happen. All unprepared when the outcomes are poor, even when the outcome has little to do with them and all to do with what brought the patient to them in the first place." The whole team is impacted as the members try to repair the patient in a struggle against death. And, Nenner says, when life is no longer a possibility, the trauma team's focus turns to when death will come. The members try to revive the patient long enough for a mother or father to say good-bye. The timing of the death is in the hands of the doctors. Having a small period of time with a loved one is little consolation, but so many never have even this chance. For the trauma team, it is a small victory.

Just being there, it might appear or feel as if you are doing nothing. In reality, the only thing that could make the situation better is if you could turn back time and undo the traumatic event. Facilities such as Lutheran Medical Center in Brooklyn often offer a family its first exposure to a trained support system. Asking for help and guidance will provide you with information on how to cope with your circumstances and put you in touch with professionals who can further guide you.

### What to Do and Say

Fred Nenner's comments illustrate the uncertainty that surrounds trauma and the need for knowledge about how to handle these special conditions with great flexibility. How you start is critical.

- First," Nenner says, "let's talk about rules. There are none." We must not have any preconceived notions or any preset plan. We cross every bridge when we come to it.
- We must listen in a special way, often in a more intuitive way than anything else.
- We must identify existing and potential members

who can make up the best support system, which will include parents, family members, social workers, religious advisors, school counselors, and other professionals. (These people may need to be contacted quickly.)

### What to Avoid

- We must not make false reassurances.
- We must not fall into the trap of trying to take away the pain.
- We must avoid trying to explain the loss in either religious or philosophical terms too soon.

---

## ONE PERSONAL EXPERIENCE OF TRAUMA

There are many who have directly and indirectly contributed to this material. Their contributions serve as a message that survival is possible. The following contribution is from Dr. Lisa Hudson, Ph.D., who is a psychologist, and describes in a very personal way how she recovered from a life-changing, traumatic event.

When I went to bed on the night of October 22, 1983, my life was stable, predictable, safe, and happy. Within twenty-four hours, I would wake to find my world toppled, shattered into a million pieces. That world, and I, and my son's life, would never be the same again.

There is nothing that can prepare you or your children when sudden, traumatic death comes. But there are things you can do to help yourself cope better. Then, you can help your children cope with what I call "the bad news."

My husband was a physician in the U.S. Navy and he had been deployed with the U.S. Marine peacekeeping force in Beirut, Lebanon, in May of 1983. He left on my first Mother's Day, which was traumatic enough, but I had no idea of the trauma that lay in front of me—that seven months later, after seven months of waiting for him to come home, I would face more pain and trauma than I ever thought humanly possible to endure. And the truth is, it is more than you believe you can endure. That is the nature of trauma.

On the morning of October 23, 1983, I awoke to the bad news: that the Marine Corps barracks where my husband lived, had been bombed in the worst non-nuclear explosion in U.S. history. A truck on a suicide mission had detonated inside their building, killing 241 soldiers as they slept. As with any traumatic event, that day is frozen in my mind, as if someone took a picture, scanned it, and put those scenes, sights, smells, sounds, and emotions in my head, to be imprinted there forever.

It is as if the brain remembers everything associated with the event—even if you don't—and can recall certain aspects of the trauma without having to be there.

Things can happen years later, and you feel as if you are "back there," reliving it all over again—as if someone pushed the "play" button on the VCR as it replays all the emotions recorded on the trauma tape. Your "reliving" experiences may or may not even resemble the original trauma, but something will trigger the old, imprinted memory of the trauma—and the tape will begin to play.

That fateful morning, after hearing the bad news, I began a waiting process—part of the trauma, that for me, became a significant aspect of the trauma process, and would years later become one of many "triggers" for me.

Years later, when placed in a situation where I was waiting to hear important "news"—news that could alter the course of my life again—a grade in graduate school, whether or not a relationship was going to continue or end, a reply from an important letter, an answer about anything that I perceived as critical to my life's direction, I would become severely anxious, and relive the same feelings I had once felt when waiting on the original bad news. It was a reenactment of the old trauma but was technically unrelated to it. However, because my brain remembered, it felt exactly the same.

That morning, I remember feeling a wash of emotions: mostly terror, fear, panic, anxiety, worry, confusion. I couldn't sleep or eat. I felt numb and detached from my world, alone and abandoned, as if I was going to die. I cried plenty, but it was a deep groaning, a wailing, not the kind of tears you cry when you feel depressed and sad. I was dreadfully afraid—like waiting for a bomb to fall on me too, but I didn't know when it was coming.

I wanted answers but dreaded them at the same time. I remember only certain details about that week and almost have amnesia about the rest. The parts that stand out are those that were the most painful or traumatic: when I turned on the TV and saw the grisly scene; when I got the news that he was MIA (missing in action); seeing my aunt and mother caring for my baby because I felt totally incapacitated; when I got the news that he was dead.

I can recall the details: where I was, how I was lying on the bed, how the doorbell sounded, how my father's footsteps sounded coming down the hall, how his face looked when he told me the news, how I felt numb, but relieved—it was over.… That was seventeen years ago—and I can remember as if it were yesterday. That first year following my husband's death, I believe I had Post-Traumatic Stress Disorder, a disorder that is characterized by psychological state of numbness and detachment, yet filled with anxiety which can manifest itself in insomnia, irritability, hypervigilance (a constant state of alarm).

Instead of falling apart, I became very functional—which not only helped me cope, but also enabled me to survive. I seemed to be grieving—I cried a lot, I felt a lot of emotional pain and loss, pining for my husband and the life I once had, but for the most part, I kept the terror, the unbearable fear buried inside. Keeping all this buried was the only way I could keep going. If I let the feelings have full reign, I didn't think I could cope with also being a parent, with all its demands and responsibilities.

I knew I had a baby to care for, and that being a depressed mother could lead to a depressed child. So I shut off my emotions in order to parent, and got very, very busy. I pretended to be okay a lot of the time. But I was really in shock for the most part of two years. I was not okay. I actually postponed my traumatic reactions and some of my own grief until years later when he was older, when I felt like I could "let go."

Another part of this that was actually detrimental to me was that others around me were encouraging me to "go on" when inside I wasn't ready to go on.

I was trying to process what had happened and all the emotions that accompany such a traumatic loss. They also encouraged me "not to think about it," or "put it behind me." What I really needed was to think about it, and talk about it, and let my insides "scream" for a while—release the pain, so I could heal. Instead, all the busyness and avoidance just put a crude scab on a really infected wound.

The second year after his death, I became extremely depressed and hopeless. Going back over the trauma was not something I thought about doing, and even seemed impossible because others seemed to expect me to be "over it" by now. Talking about the details of the event seemed foolish, and I would become embarrassed or seem "weak" if I talked about it. It was as if others expected me to avoid talking about it or him, and if I did, I would be crazy. If they only knew, I felt crazy inside not talking about it.

### What Helped Me

Talking it out. Talk and talk and talk to someone who will listen, patiently and nonjudgmentally. That may be a friend, a counselor, a minister. A therapist trained in trauma recovery would be an excellent choice. Or another person who has "been there" can be very helpful. Those who have been through a similar experience can speak your language and really say "I understand." Reviewing the details: talk about them: what you saw, heard, did, didn't do, where you were, what was going on around the trauma, what you felt. Allowing my deepest, darkest, most painful, horrible feelings to be expressed, even if they are overwhelming. At times they were overwhelming for me.

There are no rules about recovering from trauma.

Be yourself, and let yourself say or feel anything you legitimately feel.

Be honest about what you feel—there is nothing bad or wrong to feel.

You may find yourself resorting to former ways of coping (good and bad).

This is called regression. It can be seen in forms of dependency to people, substances such as alcohol, drugs, or food.

Letting yourself feel and express anger is very important. After a traumatic loss, your sense of justice and fairness, your set of assumptions about life, change. There can be tremendous anger at others, at the person who died, at those you thought could have prevented it, at yourself, at your children, at God.

Use any and all resources at your disposal: a support group, Internet resources to chat with others who have suffered a traumatic loss, write a journal, get counseling or therapy, join a gym and get exercise. Aerobic activity has been documented to reduce anxiety and help with trauma recovery.

Make time for yourself. Spend time in quiet. Meditate, pray, read, use guided imagery or relaxation. Walk. Jog. Get a massage. Be with people who comfort you, not those who push you. Know that you may feel more irritable, sleep less, get angry easier over little things, be more impatient. Allow time to pass because you have the task of a dual recovery. At first you must deal with the trauma, then the grief.

Trauma is different from grief in that there is much anxiety and damage to your emotions, as if someone stabbed your heart a million times AND ripped it out.

Avoid stressful situations as much as possible, and simplify your life.

Have realistic expectations of yourself and your children. Your life cannot and will not operate the way it did before the loss, so don't expect everything to go smoothly, nor for you or your children to behave the way they once did.

Until there is time for healing, everyone will be reacting and acting in unpredictable and often confusing ways.

Let yourself and your children know that trauma does not have a quick cure.

### A Child's Experience

My son's experience has been unique. He never knew his father, yet he has experienced the grief of absence, growing up without a father. It surfaced first when he went to first grade, when he recognized that other boys had dads that went fishing with them, did Cub Scout projects and campouts, let them help around the house, played football in the backyard.

It surfaced again between his sixteenth and seventeenth year, following another loss. He actually grieved for a life he dreamed of, a father he never knew and wished to know, for being without a father to do things with, share his life, to guide him, to be proud of and to imitate. He began to desire to be more like him, even deciding to become a doctor, like his father.

He wanted to see pictures, newspaper articles, and magazine articles about the event. We got out letters he wrote so he could see his handwriting, read his words. He even tried on his shoes. He wanted to be with his friends more, and he wanted to talk to them about it. He withdrew from me. He cried and mourned, and of course, I felt a resurgence of my own grief when he was going through his. I had to find ways to take care of myself.

### What May Help Your Children

1. Encourage but don't force them to talk—to you, a trusted friend, a clergyperson. If the details of their trauma distress you, get extra help from a therapist trained to work with victims of trauma.

2. Let them draw about their feelings. Art is one way children process their feelings of trauma and emotional pain. From their drawings, you may even learn what particular aspects of the trauma is most distressing them.

3. Let them play out their feelings. One friend of mine whose husband had died in a plane crash had a four-year-old son who would play with toy airplanes and have them "crash." This play-acting out of this trauma would trigger a flood of emotions and cause her significant distress while he was doing this. She recognized it was his way of processing the trauma. So, she would leave the room, but let him keep playing out his feelings.

4. Help them develop rituals to remember the person who died.

5. It's okay for them to see you cry and mourn. That gives them permission and freedom to do the same. It's not good for you to hold everything in, or pretend everything is ok, because they won't feel safe or that it's ok to let their feelings show.

6. It's not good for children to feel abandoned by you too. If you find yourself isolating yourself too much or not being there for them, you need to seek help.

Try not to become involved in intense new or intimate relationships too soon after a traumatic loss. It may distract you from your pain and make you feel better temporarily, but will take important time and attention away from your priority: yourself and your children. They need and depend on you to be available emotionally and physically for them. They cannot do it for themselves. They need to feel secure and safe by you being there for them. If you take care of their smaller fires now, you won't be putting out a bigger fire later. If you aren't emotionally and physically available for your children when the trauma and loss occurs, you will pay a higher price later.

7. Know that you will probably have a higher need for control than ever before, because a trauma leaves you feeling so out of control. You have experienced something unanticipated. You may find yourself being overprotective for a while. Communicate this to your children and why you may need more reassurance of their whereabouts than before.

8. Communicate often to your children that they are loved, wanted, and needed. Hold and touch them frequently. They may feel much more afraid than ever, and the world feels just as unsafe to them or more so than you.

9. Let them know it is not their fault.

10. Provide information as is necessary.

11. Keep the child a part of the family unit. Don't send them away from the home too much. They need to be a part of the process, the support, and the healing process.

12. If you need a break, locate resources to help you find time for yourself. Arrange sitters, family or friends to keep your children for a few hours every week or even an hour each day at first when you need to decompress.

13. Most importantly, get help for yourself first. You cannot help your children unless you help yourself.

14. Do not depend or rely on your children to be your sounding board. They do not need to feel responsible for

helping you cope. It is too much of a burden for them. Get your own counselor, and try to journal your feelings or save your most problematic emotional conflicts until you meet with your counselor. It frightens children to see a parent hysterical or losing control. They feel there will be no one to take care of them.

Be aware that a grief reaction may surface years later in children as they go through different developmental stages of understanding the loss. Don't think something is necessarily wrong with their need to process their loss at different times in their life. Get professional help if other aspects of their life seem affected (school performance, peer relationships, conduct, mood changes, behavior changes, developing nervous habits like nail biting, hair pulling, bed wetting, picking at their skin, angry outbursts, headaches, stomachaches, frequent physical complaints, isolation). After one year following a trauma, many children show few or no symptoms. It is not uncommon to observe symptoms reoccurring years later when they are reminded of or confronted with situations which resurface their loss.

### What to Say/Not Say to a Traumatized Person

DO say:

1. "Tell me what happened if you feel like talking," and then be willing to hear the details. They may need to tell the same story or part of the story over and over again for a while.

2. Offer practical assistance like running errands, cooking, baby-sitting, grocery shopping. Say something like "Let me keep the children one afternoon for you to do something for yourself."

3. Remember that a traumatized person may look fine on the outside because they are in shock, and it doesn't mean they are okay. You might mention certain behaviors they are

showing that concern you: like "you seem to be drinking more lately" or "you seem to be so frustrated with everyone and everything. I'd like to help," or "Tell me something about how you are feeling."

4. Help them locate resources in their community and/or people trained in helping survivors of trauma. Get a mental health counselor's name, address, and telephone number and have it available. Offer to attend the first session with them if they need support.

DON'T:

1. Don't tell me to "put it out of my mind," when it is so new. I can't—it's all I can think about. Help find ways to get me out, and away from my own thoughts sometimes, doing calm, nurturing things, like walking near a pond, having a cup of coffee in a quiet coffee shop, or getting away for a weekend at a spa where I can be pampered and recharged. Trauma is draining.

2. Don't be afraid to ask me about it—I need you to ask, and if I don't want to talk I will tell you. Your bringing it up doesn't "make" me think about it—I am already thinking about it all the time.

3. Don't criticize the person's reactions or minimize the trauma by saying "it could have been worse" (because nothing feels worse than this), suggest it was God's will, minimize the person's feelings, or say you know how they feel unless you have experienced something similar.

I still believe that the best things I did to recover from the trauma were to stay close to my family, to stay busy with things I enjoyed doing, to be with others who were caring, calming, and supportive, and giving a lot of my time and energy to the upbringing of my son. Though I was traumatized and hurting, I literally immersed myself in that role—sometimes I think I just didn't know what else to do. Giving myself so fully to him and his welfare helped me find a purpose for living, gave me a diversion from the trauma and grief, and was an investment that would pay great dividends. Although I had to postpone many things in my own life—even some of my grief and trauma—until years later, such a sacrifice has paid great rewards. The only thing I would do differently is to have gotten professional help from the beginning and through the years that were so hard. It might have saved me some of the pain I felt later. Help is out there if you can recognize that you need it or want it. I thought a lot of what I was experiencing was just "normal" which it was, but what I didn't know was that I didn't have to suffer in silence about it. My friends tired of my need to talk about the trauma long before I did, so I began to suppress too much and often drifted into unhealthy ways of coping to escape and ease the burden and pain. Trauma recovery is a life-long process. Aspects of the trauma still surface from time to time even after seventeen years. But I know better how to cope with it when it does, and I know it is to be expected.

When your life has been altered in such a dramatic way, there is no other expectation that could be more realistic. I will never forget it, but I have learned to live with it, and go on. New meanings about myself and life have emerged, and my life has taken on a different view and direction. I have not escaped many painful resurgences of the trauma, but I have learned to be gentle with myself when those times come, and how to help myself. I continue to grow and learn.

What has helped me adjust to and accept my own traumatic experience is now professionally helping others with theirs—I truly do know how they feel, and can offer credible hope and help when they have lost theirs. There is no greater pain than feeling the pain of trauma and feeling so lost in it. A helping hand—whether it is from a friend or a therapist—can be the anchor in the storm, when life feels so unsafe and you feel so afraid. A combination of things helped me: time, therapy, medication, my family, my friends, going back to school, starting a new career.

Having my son gave me a reason to get up every morning. He gave me a reason for living when I had lost mine, and we have learned a lot on our journey together. He is the greatest proof that one can indeed recover from traumatic loss. In our school of trauma, he is my report card, and I think I got an A!

## Identifying Your Resources

Accept that you are dealing with an extremely difficult situation of long duration. It may be an error to assume that individuals and institutions are prepared and trained to assist with grief in general and trauma in particular. It becomes important for parents to identify resources to support themselves as well as their children. Research the strengths of your outside resources as well as their limitations.

## SCHOOLS AND TRAUMA

Is your school prepared? In "A Practical Guide To Crisis Response in Our Schools," the authors Volpe, Lerner, and Lindell point out the importance of a proactive crisis response program. As important as it is for parents to be prepared to assist their children in the event of a crisis, the importance of school preparation is on the same level. An organized and preconceived approach to intervention is more efficient and, ultimately, more effective than "thinking on the spot" and risking a haphazard crisis response. Keep in mind that the crisis may be extensive and far-reaching. Educators may find themselves assisting numerous traumatized children, over an extended period of time, while being personally affected themselves. You don't want to decide to shop for a fire extinguisher when your home is already on fire. Be prepared!

## What Might You Expect

- Regression in behavior where children act as they might at a younger age. Pre- and elementary school-children may return to thumb-sucking, bed-wetting, and fear of the dark. Traumatized children may exhibit separation anxiety, including fearing leaving their parents side.
- Increased fear and anxiety. School phobia may develop if the event was school connected.
- Decreased academic performance due to the impact of trauma and grief on the ability to concentrate and focus.
- Increased aggression and oppositional behavior as well as a decreased ability to tolerate frustration.
- Increased irritability and depressive feelings.
- Denial as a means of shutting out the impact or significance of an event.

Guidelines for Seeking Individualized Intervention

- Your child cannot engage in responsibilities and activities at home and school, after a sufficient amount of time has passed since the event and after a majority of his/her peers are able to do so.
- Your child continues to exhibit high levels of emotional responsiveness after a majority of his or her peers have discontinued doing so.

- Your child appears depressed, withdrawn, and non-communicative.
- Your child continues to exhibit poor academic performance and concentration.
- Your child expresses suicidal or homicidal ideation or is hurting him/herself.
- Your child exhibits an apparent increased usage of drugs or alcohol.
- Your child experiences significant weight gain or loss.
- Your child exhibits significant changes in behavior.
- Your child discontinues attending to his/her hygienic needs.

Dr. Robert Motta of Hofstra University suggests that the role of the school psychologist be one of coordination of services through outside agencies, in school, and at home. The school psychologist, even with adequate training in exposure and relaxation techniques, may not be able to provide the level of therapeutic coverage that is necessary. He or she, within the school environment can, along with trained teachers, provide a safe, private, nonjudgmental atmosphere where, either through individual or group counseling sessions, the child can discuss his or her fears.

# 5

## The Funeral—Finding a Way to Say Good-bye

Several years ago, in a segment on the TV show "Different Strokes," the young leading character (played by Gary Coleman) asked to be taken to his mother's grave. As he sat by the tombstone, he poured out his feelings, apologizing to her many years after her death for never having said good-bye. "They wouldn't let me come to the funeral, they thought I was too young," he said. "They thought I wouldn't understand. So I had to come now." The child wanted to make sure that his mother knew he cared.

Scenes like that don't happen when parents include their children in the rituals our culture has provided for people to express their grief. Children, like adults, need a vehicle to mourn their loss, to say good-bye and get on with living again. Families deprived of this catharsis, because their loved ones were missing in action or lost at sea, often have a hard time coming to terms with the loss. Unless they are able to face the death squarely, acknowledge the loss in some kind of ritual and bury the one they loved, the grief doesn't go away. As sociologist Alvin Toffler points out in *Future Shock*, the funeral is an important change-buffer, marking off a significant event in our lives.

With the gathering of friends, the religious services, and perhaps a procession to the place of burial, the funeral gives people a ritual in which they can start to resolve their feelings about the death. It also gives them something to do. For many years it was felt that becoming involved in the funeral preparations only made the grief worse—so very often one person in the family, "the strong one," was expected to put his or her feelings on hold and handle all the arrangements. Others appeared only when they were told to come. All that is changing now, however. These preparations are now seen by many people as an outlet for grief and anxiety.

Parents I've talked to have found that not giving their children the choice of attending the funeral, in an attempt to protect them from pain, is a tactic that can often backfire.

> It was winter in the upper midwest, and the snow lay in drifts around the college town. Debbie climbed through the snowbanks, up the steps of her dorm, and walked into the reception room. "Debbie," yelled a friend, "you got a message to call home immediately." Debbie called home; her father was dead. "I'm coming right now," she told her mother. It took nearly twenty- four hours on buses that got stuck in a blizzard, and on trains and planes, but finally she made it back to New York and walked in the door. "When's the funeral going to be?" she finally asked after the hugs and the tears. "I didn't want you to have to go through it," her mother said. "I had your father cremated this morning."

It's hard to fault that mother; she really felt that what she was doing was right. She meant well, but in the midst of the crisis she forgot that her daughter had the right to make a choice, too—to see her father before he was cremated if she wanted to.

Rabbi Earl Grollman, editor of the book *Explaining Death to Children*, says that for children the funeral service is a positive learning experience, one that helps them accept the reality of death as separation, even as they are taught about birth and maturity. "As a rite of passage, the funeral helps to instill the feeling in the child that he is part of the order of things."

Carol Smith-Torres, a chaplain at the Columbia Presbyterian Medical Center in New York City, points out that there are different ways of asking the question "Do you want to go to the funeral?" and each way sends a different message to the child.

First, you might say, "Do you really want to go?" That sends the message, "Don't come!"

Second, you might say, "You're coming to the funeral, aren't you?" That tells the child he'd better come.

Third, a parent can ask, "Would you like to come to the funeral with me?" That gives the youngster a choice.

Most people think that funerals are all alike, but the fact is that no two are ever alike. I know, because as a funeral director, I've been involved in thousands of them. Just as people are different and families are different, so are the ways they say good-bye to their loved ones.

Reverend Doug Manning, in *A Minister Speaks About Funerals*, suggests that within each funeral, the family should have a "private time," an hour or so in which they sit down as a group and swap stories about the one they loved. It's much like the Jewish custom of "sitting shiva." When a person dies, it matters to the other family members that his or her life had significance. In this private time, the family deals with this significance, relating stories about how the dead person touched their lives. It gives everyone a license to discuss both the good times and the bad. While they're sitting there, the children will learn how to handle themselves in their grief; they'll see that it's okay to express negative feelings or even to laugh in the midst of grief.

## TELLING CHILDREN
## WHAT TO EXPECT

Should children be allowed to come to the funeral home? Definitely—but they must be prepared first about what to expect. Whether they're preschoolers or teenagers, whether they're self-possessed or timid, they should be carefully schooled on what they'll be seeing. Then they can make an informed choice about whether to go to the funeral home or not. Walking in cold on a situation you've never experienced before—especially a scene charged with this kind of emotion—can be terribly unnerving.

Many hospital personnel realize the importance of preparing children for what to expect. Several years ago, my youngest son went in for surgery. On the day he went into the hospital, we were taken on a tour of the operating room and intensive care, the recovery room, and the room where he'd be staying. A nurse showed him how she gives injections by using a doll; he was given a face mask to play jet pilot with so he wouldn't be alarmed when it came time for the anesthesia; the whole experience was made very familiar to him. Later, as each procedure was performed, there were no surprises.

I propose that the same consideration be given to a child coming to a funeral. No matter what age he is, the youngster should be told what to expect—the size of the room, the fact that there may be a lot of flowers, who will be coming and how they will probably be dressed, how long the child will stay, when he must leave, and why. (Adults need some time for themselves.)

To a young child you might say something like: "Grandpa's going to be in a big room with a green rug and yellow wallpaper, and there will be paintings on the wall and lots of flowers around the casket. Grandpa will be lying down in the casket, which is a box that they bury Grandpa in so that no dirt gets on him [this is important to many children]. Grandpa's casket is silver and he's dressed in his dark blue suit, and he'll be lying down and not moving, because his body doesn't work anymore. He'll still look the same — just very still. When we go in, a lot of people will be standing and sitting around and some of them will be crying because they're so sad that Grandpa died. And if you want to, you can come in the room where Grandpa will be and say a prayer or say good-bye to Grandpa. He won't be able to hear you because his body isn't working, but if there's something special that you want to leave in the casket with Grandpa, a flower or something, you can do that."

As always, you must change this explanation to fit your particular family customs and religious traditions. The important thing is that the experience should be described as fully as possible.

The message must be structured very carefully — never assume that your child understands what you do. One little boy was given a very detailed explanation of how Grandpa's body would be brought from the hospital to the funeral home. Then he was asked, "Do you want to go to the funeral home to see Grandpa?" "No," the child replied. "How come?" "I don't want to see Grandpa without his arms and legs and head." Where did he ever get such an idea? "Well, when Mommy gives me a bath, she tells me to wash my arms and legs and head, and then wash my body, and Daddy said they were bringing Grandpa's *body* to the funeral home."

Many people, when they hear that story, are surprised that a child would have that reaction. But such misunderstandings are common. When you're talking about the dead person, use his or her name, not the word "body." Don't assume that a child knows that when a body is in a casket, it's lying down. One youngster came into the funeral home and got very upset because Grandpa wasn't sitting up like he was the last time he saw him. Don't assume, either, that children know that a dead body doesn't move or that a person really is inside the casket when it's closed. Children often believe only what they see, and if they see only the head and torso of the body, they often think the other half is missing or that the body is a fake. It is important to confront this issue gently. I suggest saying to your child, "Some children think that only half a person is there—if you want, we can have the funeral director open the bottom half and show you his legs. . . ." Let them touch the dead person if they want to.

One young fellow pulled up his father's sleeve, saw his tattoo, and said, "That's Daddy, all right!" Eighty-five percent of the children I ask say yes, they do want to have the casket opened all the way so they can see that the lower half of the body is there. It's better than letting their imaginations go wild.

As I've said, the child should be given a choice, after the explanations have been made, as to whether he wants to go to the funeral home, the funeral service, and/or the cemetery. Never force him to go to any of them. Also, never push him into doing something he doesn't want to do, such as walking up and touching the body at the funeral home, even if everyone else is doing it. Always allow him to change his mind, even at the last minute.

If your child doesn't want to go to the service, try to get him or her to talk about it. Sometimes they have their reasons. Elizabeth said she didn't want to have as the last image in her mind a grandfather who was dead—she wanted to remember him as he was when she last saw him, playing baseball with the kids in the park. That was her choice and it should be respected. But if your children want to come and say good-bye, they should be given that right, too.

Children often handle crises better than we adults do, especially when they're equipped with the right information. Even a child of four or five, if he has a certain amount of self-discipline, should be allowed to come to the funeral home for a short visit, if he wants to. Children in the early school years can be expected to sit quietly for up to half an hour. Parents can ask that a special time be set aside for young children to visit the funeral home—so that they can avoid the busy times and be able to devote themselves to answering their children's questions. Especially if the person who died is their parent, young children should be allowed to see the dead person for a moment or two, because unless they have some memory of the body at the funeral they may have trouble believing that their loved one is actually dead.

It's important, though, not to leave the child alone by the casket. Dr. Hal Fishkin remembers going to the funeral home to see a friend who died. When he walked in he asked where his friend's 16-year-old son was. "Oh, he's in there with his mother," Fishkin was told. The boy had been sitting beside his dead mother for half an hour and no one had wanted to disturb him. "I walked in and the boy was sitting there. So I said to him, 'Come on, let's go.' And he came along. He was glad that someone had come in and told him to leave." Children need to be told what to do sometimes. When they're upset, they need someone to help them get themselves back together.

If a child is surrounded by sensible adults and allowed to talk out his feelings, he'll usually handle the time at the funeral home just fine. Very often he'll find the ritual fascinating, learn from the experience, and come out of it feeling supported, part of the group. The adults are the ones who set the limits and control what is going to happen in this crisis. If the adults behave honestly, calmly, and lovingly, the children will respond in kind.

## A GOOD-BYE GIFT

Many parents find that a simple "good-bye gift" is an effective way to help their child realize the finality of death, and perform one last act of recognition and respect. I suggest to parents that when they're making funeral arrangements they let their children order the kind of flowers Grandma would have liked, or choose some of the music. Some youngsters make a last gift to be put in the casket—a drawing or a note saying how much they loved the person who died. I've seen little kids pull dandelions out of the backyard and stick them in Grandpa's hand in the casket. They may have looked like weeds to us, but to the little ones they were something significant . . . an appropriate way to say "I love you." Make sure, though, that the child who writes a letter or puts a gift in the casket understands that the dead person can't read or see or use the present.

When saying good-bye, a youngster needs a license to do what he thinks is best. One 13-year-old boy, whose grandfather was his baseball coach, put his prized baseball trophy in the casket. Many members of the family thought that was a terrible idea, but the boy's parents went along with his wish. They pointed out to him that there was no getting it back; but if that's what he wanted, it was okay with them. They acknowledged him and accepted his decision.

Sometimes children and adults need a keepsake to remind them of their deceased loved one. When a family refuses to move anything out of the dead person's room—to preserve it as a kind of shrine—that can be dangerous, an unhealthy form of bonding in an attempt to idealize the dead person. But keeping a little remembrance can be a good thing.

Mark Oberman wrote an article for *Newsday Magazine* about what it was like when his infant son died. In the story, he described how his father had "stolen" a pair of the child's sneakers and kept them alongside his own shoes on the floor of his closet. Finally, the father gave his son one of the sneakers. "Since we made that poignant exchange, I, too, keep that one little blue sneaker on the floor of my clothes closet along with my shoes. Somehow, it gives me great comfort. It helps me, in a small way, to accept his life and his death. To enjoy the child in me. To live more fully in the present."

Some parents arrange for the children to have their own little service, which the children plan themselves and to which they invite whoever they like. This is often a good time to answer questions and straighten out misconceptions. One little boy who was told that Grandpa can now see God in heaven thought that Grandpa's body may be here, but his eyes were in heaven. Another got really upset that Grandma was being buried in the ground. "Isn't it cold down there?" His parents returned to their explanation of what "dead" means and said that Grandma couldn't be cold because her body had stopped working and she couldn't feel anything anymore. Talking it out gives them a chance to verbalize their feelings and absorb the shock of the death.

## QUESTIONS YOUR CHILD MIGHT ASK

Preteens and teenagers will often be interested in the mechanics of the wake or funeral. Here are some questions and answers that might help you respond to their curiosity.

Q: What is a wake?

A: Before a person is buried, many people like to gather in the presence of the dead person and talk about him or her. They do this to pay their respects to both the dead person and his survivors. This custom is also known as "calling hours."

Q: If the body is dead, why does it need to be preserved?

A: A dead body will decompose very quickly. So it needs to be embalmed so that it can be viewed by visitors. That means that certain chemicals are injected into the body, like a transfusion, to preserve it until it's buried. The body is cleaned and the hair is washed. The openings of the body are disinfected and closed so that fluids won't leak out. If parts of the body were damaged as a result of injury or disease, they are specially treated and restored.

Q: Why can't they leave the person's body alone when they die? Why do they have to put make-up on him and make him look phony?

A: No one is trying to make the person look like he did not die. The people at the funeral home just try to make the dead person look like he did when he was alive, so that his loved ones will have a nicer image to remember.

Q: Why do people send flowers? Isn't it a waste, since the
   dead person can't see them.
A: People send flowers to show the dead person's family that
   the person was important to them. Flowers are appropriate not only because they are beautiful, but because
   they symbolize life and death. In place of flowers, some
   families prefer donations to a favorite charity.

Q: What is cremation?
A: Cremation is a process by which a dead body is burned
   and turned into ashes. Sometimes the ashes are stored
   in a special jar called an urn, sometimes they're buried,
   and sometimes they're scattered over the ground or the
   ocean.

After a child has the answers to his questions, he'll probably want to know how to act at the funeral. Perhaps a friend
of the family or a schoolmate died. Explain that when he
goes to visit the family at the funeral home, he should just
be himself. It's not necessary to say much. Whatever you do
say, the more personal and heartfelt, the better. Tell the
child if he wants to talk about things he remembers about
the dead person, that would be fine. Or he might even talk
about how sad he feels or angry that the person died; that
will let the family know how much he cares. Let him know
that if he feels like crying, that's okay. Knowing that other
people are grieving too lightens the load. And just being a
good listener can do a world of good.

When we talk about death, we get in touch with life.
Sometimes in our day-to-day routine we get so caught up in
doing things that we forget what's really important . . . our
beliefs, our dreams, the ones we love. But when we talk
about death and, for a moment, confront the fact that no

one's going to live forever, that we're only here for a little while, we strip away the trappings of our lives and get to the core of what we feel and believe. As we realize how precious it is to be alive, we become more human. How wonderful it is if we can share that moment with our children.

## Healing

### LIFE GOES ON
#### BY
#### PAT TRAVIS ROSENBERG

*Four years have passed. In a second's thought I can
    be back to the*
*Beginning of this journey…riding in a car, driving
    into a nightmare.*

*For four years I have been searching for
    understanding and truth…*
*I watched nature.*
*Felt nature.*
*Heard nature.*
*Slipped into nature.*
*In my journey to understand my loss, I have found
    ground and a road to enlightenment, acceptance,
    and truth.*

*Four years have passed. There were seasons that
    changed without recognition like a boat lost in fog.*
*There were moments that were so crystal clear they
    seem mummified petroglyphs.*

*I know sorrow and missing never go away—perhaps
    there is always an empty spot within the inner soul.*

*I also learned I can hold on to living without devastation; that accepting is continuing without letting go of what was precious.*

*Life is a constant current, flowing but always in flux—we must accept this, and follow our journey.*

# Crisis Checklist

This section is intended to serve as a quick reference to the information given in more detail throughout the book. Here you will find, in outline form, the parts of the "message" that you want to send to your children. As I said before, not everything here will apply to your particular situation; you will have to pick and choose from the information offered here. Remember also that although this material is directed toward explaining the death of a person, you can take a similar approach when you're explaining the death of a pet.

I hope that this section will prove useful to you during a crisis, or any time you need a ready answer to a specific question or situation, and that you will also refer back to the first four chapters for more of this information and the impact it can have on your children. Few people in crisis will have the energy to read the whole book at that time; understanding this and, at the same time, acknowledging your own need will help you help your children.

When you confront the problem of telling your children about the death.

1. Accept that it's not easy. You may:
   - *be upset and stressed*
   - *lack energy*
   - *feel unable to concentrate*
   - *worry about how your emotions will affect your child*
   - *be concerned about the effect of the death on your child*
   - *want to protect your child from pain*
   - *not know how much your child understands about death*

2. Be prepared for resistance from others. People may say of your children:
   - *They don't know what's going on.*
   - *Wait until later to tell them.*
   - *Make up a story.*
   - *Don't say anything.*
   - *Send them away until the funeral is over.*
   - *Why do you want to put them through this?*

Consider saying to these people:
   - *I really could use your help; I believe that what I am doing is the right thing for my children and me.*
   - *You can help me by reinforcing what I am telling them, or by saying nothing, Don't undermine my effort.*

Parents should know that children will:
   - *read emotions around them*
   - *respond to body language*

- *overhear conversations*
- *ask questions directly or indirectly.*

Your children will receive some kind of message, no matter what you do; *it is impossible not to communicate.* They will see your grief and if you have not explained what's going on, it will signal to them that something is the matter. They will be confused and anxious.

*Control* the message instead by giving them accurate information, geared for the age of the child, in language he or she can understand.


## UNDERSTANDING SADNESS

1. Your children need to know:
   - *why you are sad*
   - *why others are sad*
   - *why they are sad*

Acknowledging this lets your children know that it's *okay* to be sad. Tell them, "This is how we feel when someone dies."

2. Children must be told that it is the death that has made you sad. Without an explanation, they may think your sadness is caused by something they did or didn't do. Start by saying:
   - *"This is a very, very sad time . . ."*
   - *"A very, very sad thing has happened . . ."*
   - *"Mommy and Daddy are sad because . . ."*

## UNDERSTANDING "DEAD" AND WHAT IT MEANS

1. Explain that *dead* means that:
   - *A person's body has stopped working and won't work anymore.*
   - *The body won't do any of the things it used to do: it won't talk, walk, move, see, or hear; none of the parts work.*
   - *The person won't feel any of the feelings he or she used to feel, such as sad, mad, happy, hurt, hot, or cold.*
   - *The person will not eat, drink, or go to the bathroom (urinate and defecate) anymore.*

2. Refer back to this explanation when answering questions that arise, such as:
   - *Will Grandpa ever move again? (No, his body has stopped working.)*
   - *Why can't they fix him? (Once the body stops working, it can't start again.)*
   - *Why is he cold? (The body only stays warm when it's working, like ours.)*
   - *Why isn't he moving? (He can't move because his body isn't working anymore.)*
   - *When will he come back? (He won't. People who die don't come back.)*
   - *Is he sleeping? (No. When we sleep our body is still working, just resting.)*
   - *Can he hear me? (No. He could only hear you if his body was working.)*

- *Can he eat after he's buried? (No, a person eats only when his body is working.)*

3. Don't use words like "passed away," "left us," "gone on"; to a child this sounds like the person is taking a trip. His parents' trips may then become a source of anxiety, if the child thinks that some people never return from them. Don't hold out any hope of return; death is a form of abandonment.

## SPECIAL CHARACTERISTICS TO KEEP IN MIND

### NEWBORN TO AGE THREE

1. No matter how young the child, he or she can sense when things in the family routine are different. However, they will not be able to figure out why they are different. Among the changes in the daily routine that children might sense are:
- *excitement at home*
- *sadness or anxiety*
- *presence of new people*
- *parents being gone at odd times*
- *a significant person in their lives is missing*

2. Watch your child to see if he or she starts acting differently. Among the changes you might note are:
- *stopped or altered nursing patterns (in infants)*
- *crankiness*

- *altered sleep patterns*
- *change in eating habits*

3. Children in this age group cannot comprehend the concept of death; however, they can understand sadness. When you know what changes to look for in your children, you can respond more sensitively to their needs.

### AGE THREE TO SIX

1. Children in this age group think death is reversible: people will come back; death isn't forever. E.T. came back from the dead; also Jesus and Lazarus. The coyote on the Roadrunner cartoon program gets right back up again after being squashed.

They will ask questions about the dead person's return; also, they may not be really affected by the death, since they expect the person to come back soon. They cannot understand the concept of "finality" at this age.

2. They will connect events that don't belong connected:
- *Does this mean someone else is going to die?*
- *Grandpa died from a headache; Mommy says she has a headache too. . . .*
- *Old people die; Daddy is very old; Daddy may die too. . . .*

Be prepared for indirect questions, aimed at finding out if someone else might die: "How old are you? How old is Daddy?"

You must explain the difference between:

- *very, very sick and just "sick"*
- *very, very old and over 20*
- *very old and very sick, and very old and not sick*

3. It's important that your child not assume he is responsible in any way for the death. See page 186 of the crisis checklist.

4. Explain about the emotions your child may be feeling or observing:
- *Crying is okay for everyone (boys, too).*
- *Feeling bad inside is okay. After a while, you'll feel better.*
- *Being mad is okay.*
- *People in the family might have trouble sleeping or eating; this is a natural reaction.*

## AGE SIX TO NINE

1. Most children in this age group will understand that death is final; but some might still think that the dead person will come back.

2. Children in this age group need a more detailed explanation of why the person died. It's important to distinguish fatal illness from just being sick ("It's not like when your stomach hurts, or when Mommy gets a cold . . ."). They may have a greater fear of their parents' dying, particularly if they see them as vulnerable (often ill, etc.). This concern is even greater when they are being raised by a single parent.

3. They see death as a taker; something that comes and gets you. Or they may see it as something you catch, like a cold. They also may not want to go to a house where someone has died.

4. Explain about the emotions your child may be feeling or observing:
- *Crying is okay for everyone (boys, too).*
- *Feeling bad is okay.*
- *Feeling frightened is okay.*
- *Being angry is okay.*
- *Feeling that something is missing is okay.*

Parents often find it helpful to share some of their own feelings with their children; it helps start discussion.

5. Because children in this age group connect death with violence, they may ask when being told about a death, "Who killed him?"

6. Make sure your child does not feel responsible for the death in any way; see page 186 of the crisis checklist.

## AGE NINE TO TWELVE

1. Children in this age group are more aware of the finality of death and of the impact that a death may have on them—even to the point where it affects family security and economic security.

These feelings are quite close to those experienced by adults, and parents say it helps to share their own thought and feelings with their children.

2. Children may show more anger, guilt, and grief. See pages 184–186 in the crisis checklist.

## TEENAGERS

1. The older your children, the greater the temptation to assume they can handle themselves and their problems. *Don't assume this*; they need your help and support to understand their feelings at this time.

Check especially pages 184-186 in the crisis checklist.

## DESCRIBING HOW/WHY THE DEATH OCCURRED (TO YOUNG CHILDREN)

1. Old Age
   - *"When a person gets very, very, very old, his body wears out and stops working. . . ."*

2. Terminal Illness (for example, cancer or AIDS)
   - *"Because the disease couldn't be stopped, the person got very, very sick; his body wore out and stopped working. . . ."*

3. Accident
   - *"A terrible thing happened (car crash, etc.); his body was badly hurt and couldn't be fixed. It stopped working. . . ."*

4. Miscarriage
   - *"Sometimes when a baby is just starting to grow,*

*something happens that makes it stop. We don't
know what it was; it wasn't anything anyone did. . . ."*

## 5. Stillborn
- *"Sometimes something makes a baby die before it is
born. We're not sure why, but it's nothing anybody
did or didn't do. . . ."*

## 6. Sudden Infant Death Syndrome (SIDS)
- *"Sometimes with little babies something makes their
bodies stop working. It's nothing anybody did or forgot to do. Doctors are not sure why it happens. . . ."*

## 7. Suicide—Absolute (when there is no doubt the person killed himself)
- *"Some people's bodies get sick and just don't work
right; and sometimes a person's mind doesn't work
right. They can't see things clearly and they feel the
only way to solve their problems is to take their
lives—to kill themselves. However, this is never a solution to problems; the only reason they thought of it
is that they weren't thinking very clearly. . . ."*

## 8. Suicide—Questionable
- *"Sometimes people take pills to relax or to sleep.
Sometimes they forget how many they took and think
they need more. These pills make a person's body
slow down. Too many of them make the body stop
working. We don't think the person wanted to die,
but that's what happened. . . ."*

## 9. Homicide
- *"Sometimes very bad people do very bad things. . . ."*

## AFTER THE DEATH—
## WHAT WILL HAPPEN NOW

1. Children should be told what is going to happen and what they are going to experience. Should they be brought to the funeral home and/or service? Definitely—if they are well prepared in advance. Tell them what will happen, then give them the choice of going or not. Fit the following explanation around your family's plans and special traditions:

"_____ will be taken from _____, where he died, to the funeral home. At the funeral home _____ will be dressed in clothes that he liked and put into a casket. A casket is a box we use so that when _____is buried, no dirt will get on him. Because _____'s body isn't working anymore, it won't move or do any of the things it used to do. But it will look like _____always did.

People will come and visit us and say how sorry they are that _____ died. After _____ days the casket will be closed and taken to church, where people will say prayers for _____. Then we will go to the cemetery, where _____ will be buried in a place that _____ picked out.

If you like, you can come to the funeral home and visit for a while—even go to the cemetery. You could bring something to leave with _____ if you want; that would be nice.

We have to go to the funeral home to make plans, and we'll let you know all about them when we come back. We will be gone _____ hours."

For a cremation, use this additional information:

> "After we leave the funeral home, _____ will be taken to a crematory, a place where his body will be turned into ashes. Then we will take those ashes and _____ (scatter them; keep them in an urn). Since _____'s body doesn't work and doesn't feel anything, being cremated doesn't hurt."
>
> If the dead person has changed because of illness or accident, it's important to describe some of this change. ("It's still Grandpa, but you know he was sick and lost a lot of weight—so he will look thinner. . . .")

2. Describe the room in the funeral home where the person will be. Be very detailed and specific for younger children.
- *color of rug*
- *color of walls*
- *whether there are plants and paintings*
- *where the casket will be*
- *color and type of casket (wood, metal)*
- *color of the suit and tie, or dress, that the person will be wearing*
- *color of flowers*

3. Explain that the person will be
- *lying down*
- *not moving*
- *whether the whole body will be visible or not*

If you plan to have a closed casket, when possible suggest the children be allowed to briefly look at the whole body so they'll realize that the person is, in fact, dead and in the casket. If the casket is going to be half open, children may think that only half of the person is there; show them that this is not so. You might say, "Some children think that only half of the person is there—so if you want, we can ask the funeral director to open the bottom and show you his legs." When there is a full open casket, children will see the whole person and know that he or she is there.

4. Ask your child whether he or she wants to come to the service or not. Some children do; others don't. Remember that:

- *If a child is left out there is no next time/no going back.*
- *The child remembers not being able to say good-bye; not being included; not being given the choice.*

Telling a child what is happening and making him part of things, or asking him if he wants to be a part of things, draws him in. He makes the decision.

## HOW CHILDREN MAY REACT

Children may
- *be very upset, picking up on the family's emotion*
- *be upset about not knowing what is happening*
- *not be upset at all; or be upset only for a little while (they may think that the person will be dead only for a time, then come back)*
- *act out difficult behaviors*
- *seek attention*

- *sulk or withdraw*
- *become angry or hostile*
- *not want to believe the person is dead*
- *not want to go to the funeral, which would confirm the death*
- *not want to talk about it*
- *want to join the deceased (suicide)*
- *romanticize the death*

## ANGER

Anger is common at the time of a death; it can be very damaging to the family. Understanding it and anticipating it helps parents deal with both their own and their children's anger.

Children may be angry at their parents for:
- *not telling them that the person who died was so sick*
- *spending so much time with the sick person*
- *just because they need someone to be angry with*

Children may be angry at themselves for:
- *not intervening earlier (not taking the car keys away before an accident, etc.)*
- *wishing the person would die*
- *not visiting or helping the dying person*
- *not saying "good-bye," or "I love you"*

Children may be angry at others for:
- *not taking care of the person who died (the bartender for serving him drinks; the doctors for not treating him adequately)*

- *hurting or killing the person (in the case of an accident or homicide)*

Children may be angry at the person who died for:
- *not taking care of himself or putting himself in danger*
- *leaving, dying, abandoning them*
- *causing such family upset*
- *using up the family money*
- *not telling anyone he was sick*
- *committing suicide (causing the family pain and stigma)*
- *not fighting harder against death*

Children may be angry at their brothers and sisters for:
- *no apparent reason*
- *grieving differently (some children cry, others don't)*
- *not seeming to care*
- *not wanting to talk about the death*
- *seeming more privileged (others can go to the funeral but they can't)*

GUILT

Many people feel guilt about a death. This might stem from anger—
- *How can I be angry at the person who died?*
- *How can I be alive when he's dead?*

From the feeling that you didn't do enough—
- *I should have told the rest of the family that he was sick.*
- *I should have visited him before he died.*

And from all the "shouldn't haves" —
  • *I shouldn't have left the hospital.*
  • *I shouldn't have let him drive.*
  • *I shouldn't have left him alone (suicide).*

RESPONSIBILITY

Guilt and a feeling of responsibility go hand-in-hand. Children can feel responsible for a person's death for a number of reasons:

  • *They may have been told something that they misunderstood and took to heart ("you're driving me crazy"; "you'll be the death of me yet"; "you're killing your father").*
  • *Because they often see God as a rewarder or punisher, they may feel God has punished their bad behavior by causing the person's death; also they may feel if they had prayed harder the person wouldn't have died.*
  • *They connect events that don't belong together ("If I had sent a 'get well' card maybe he wouldn't have died").*
  • *They indulge in magical thinking ("If I wish hard enough, he'll come back"; "I got mad and wished that he would die").*

This is why it is so important that children understand why the person died. Remember, your child may think he is responsible for the death, and tell him this is not so.

In the case of *actual* responsibility for a death — parents cannot make a child believe what he or she knows to be false; parents of children directly responsible for the death of another should strongly consider professional help.

# Bibliography and Support Groups

## SUGGESTIONS FOR FURTHER READING

*The following list was prepared by Roberta Halporn, M.A., Director of the Center for Thanatology Research and Education, and Lula M. Redmond, R.N., M.S., LMFT, among others. All of the publications in this list may be ordered from the Center. A full bibliography may be obtained by sending a stamped, self-addressed Number 10 envelope to 391 Atlantic Avenue, Brooklyn, NY 11217.*

## REFERENCES

Patterson, Paul. Quoted in "Child and Death Perspectives from Birth Through Adolescence." *Archives of the Foundation of Thanatology*. Volume 10, Number 1.

Typond, Claudia. "The Death of a Child: A Case Study." *Archives of Thanatology*. Volume 10, Number 1.

### For Adults

*General*

Attig, Thomas. *How We Grieve, Relearning the World*. New York, NY: Oxford University Press, 1996.

Bard, Morton and Sangrey, Dawn. *The Crime Victim's Book*. Secaucus, NJ: Citadel Press,1986.

Bowlby, John. *Attachment and Loss*, Vol. III. New York, NY: Basic Books, 1980.

Cornils, Stanley P. *The Mourning After: How to Manage Grief Wisely*. San Jose, CA: R & E Publishers, 1995.

Doka, Kenneth J., Ph.D., ed. *Children Mourning, Mourning Children*. Hospice Foundation of America, 1995.

———. *Disenfranchised Grief, Recognizing Hidden Sorrow*. Lexington Books, 1989.

———. ed. *Living with Grief After Sudden Loss: Suicide, Homicide, Accident, Heart Attack, Stroke*. Hospice Foundation of America, 1996.

Everstine, Diane Sullivan and Louis. *The Trauma Response, Treatment for Emotional Injury*. New York, NY: W.W. Norton & Company, 1993.

Figley, Charles R., Ph.D. *Compassion Fatigue: Secondary Traumatic Stress Disorders from Treating the Traumatized*. New York: Brunner/Mazel Publishers, 1996.

———. *Trauma and Its Wake, Vol. II*. New York: Brunner/Mazel Publishers, 1986.

Fitzgerald, Helen. *The Grieving Child: A Parent's Guide*. New York, NY: Fireside, 1992.

———. *The Grieving Teen: A Guide for Teenagers and Their Friends*. New York, NY: Simon and Schuster, 2000.

———. *The Mourning Handbook*. New York, NY: Simon & Schuster, 1995. The most comprehensive resource on the subject.

Goldman, Linda. *Breaking the Silence: A Guide to Help Children With Complicated Grief, Suicide, Homicide, AIDS, Violence, and Abuse*. Levitown, PA: Accelerated Development, 1996. A reader-friendly guide for helping children cope with complicated grief situations.

Grollman, Earl. *Concerning Death*. Boston, MA: Beacon Press, 1974. A more general approach.

Herman, Judith Lewis. *Trauma and Recovery*. New York, NY: Basic Books, 1992.

Janoff-Bulman, Ronnie. *Shattered Assumptions*. New York, NY: The Free Press, 1992.

Johnson, Joy. *Keys to Teaching Children About Death and Grief*. New York, NY: Barron's Publishing, 1999. An easy-to-read book for families and caregivers.

Klicker, Ralph L. *A Student Dies, a School Mourns.* Hemisphere Publishing, 1999. A systematic guide, written by a grief counselor, for developing a death-related crisis plan.

Kübler-Ross, Elisabeth. *On Death and Dying.* New York, NY: Macmillan, 1969. The best-known statement by a medical doctor on how denying death works in the American medical complex.

Manning, Doug. *Don't Take My Grief Away.* San Francisco, CA: HarperCollins, 1984. A warm, consoling, practical guide to coping with grief.

Meichenbaum, Donald, Ph.D. *A Clinical Handbook/Practical Therapist Manual for Assessing and Treating Adults with Post-Traumatic Stress Disorder (PTSD).* Ontario, Canada: Institute Press, 1994.

Miller, Karen. *The Crisis Manual.* Beltsville, MD: Gryphon House Books, 1995. An excellent resource for educators.

Morgan, John D., Ed. *Young People and Death.* Philadelphia, PA: Charles Press, 1991. Experts in child behavior offer practical help to families dealing with life-threatening situations and loss.

Pearlman, Laurie Anne, and Saakvitne, Karen W. *Trauma and the Therapist: Countertransference and Vicarious Traumatization in Psychotherapy with Incest Survivors.* New York, NY: W.W. Norton and Company, 1995.

Pynoos, Robert, and Eth, Spencer. *Post-Traumatic Stress Disorder in Children.* Washington, D.C.: American Psychiatric Press, 1985.

Rando, Therese. *Grief, Dying and Death: Clinical Intervention for Caregivers.* Champaign, IL: Research Press, 1984.

———. *Loss and Anticipatory Grief.* Boston, MA: Lexington Books, 1986. A fine, professional overview.

Raphael, Beverly. *The Anatomy of Bereavement.* New York, NY: Basic Books, 1983.

———. *Treatment of Complicated Mourning,* Champaign, IL: Research Press, 1993.

Redmond, Lula M. *Surviving When Someone You Love Was Murdered: A Professional's Guide to Group Grief Therapy for Families and Friends of Murder Victims.* Psychological Consultation and Educations Service, P.O. Box 6111, Clearwater, FL 34618, 1989.

Rosenberg, Pat Travers. *Flying Through Clouds.* Seacliff, NY. The poem at the end of this book is extracted from this poetry volume.

Silverman, William and Cinnamon, Kenneth. *When Mourning*

*Comes*. Northvale, NJ: Jason Aronson Publishers, 1994. A book of comfort for the grieving.

Welshons, John E. *Awakening from Grief: Finding the Road Back to Joy*. Little Falls, NY. Open Heart Publications, 1999.

*Children's Conceptions of Death*

Cook, Sarah Sheets. *Children and Dying, An Exploration and Annotated Bibliography*. New York: Center for Thanatology Research and Education, 1974. Short essays that cover children's ideas, from kindergarten to adolescence.

Gullo, Steven V.; Patterson, Paul R.; and Schowalter, John E., et al., editors. *Death and Children: A Guide for Educators, Parents, and Caregivers*. Dobbs Ferry, NY: Tappan Press, 1985. A wide-ranging anthology, by educators and psychologists with long-term experience.

*Death Education for Teachers*

Stevenson, Robert; Stevenson, Eileen; and Cohen, Janice. *Curing Death Ignorance: Death Education in Schools*. Philadelphia, Pennsylvania: Charles Press, and *What Will We Do: Preparing Schools to Deal with Crises*. Amityville, NY: Baywood Publishing Company, both 1994. Experienced death educators, Stevenson and colleagues have produced two new publications which provide practical and tested methods to help teachers coping with loss in the classroom.

*Working with Children*

Grollman, Earl. *Explaining Death to Children*. Boston, MA: Beacon Press, new edition in 1994. This classic text is being updated to include advice on issues that emerged since it was first published. The language is down to earth and demystifies the painful task.

Jewett, Claudia L., and Hadley, S. *Helping Children Cope with Separation and Loss*. MA: Bergin & Garvey Pubs., Inc., 1982. Relates the smaller issues of everyday loss to the loss of an intimate because of death.

Schiff, Harriette. *Living Through Mourning*. New York: Viking, 1986. An important book for the general reader who has lost a child, by a parent with other children who survived and triumphed over the experience.

*On the Death of an Infant*
Davis, Deborah L. *Empty Cradle, Broken Heart: Surviving the Death of Your Baby.* Golden, CO: Fulcrum Publishers, 1992. A bereaved mother evokes the grief of an unconsolable loss, but describes how she and others managed to create a new vision for themselves.
Johnson, Joy and Marv. *Children Die, Too.* Omaha, NE: Centering Corp., 1978. A short pamphlet to be used during the initial shock of learning that a child might die.


*Loss of a Parent*

*For Adults*
Myers, Edward. *When Parents Die: A Guide for Adults.* New York: Penguin, 1986. A counselor talks about the issues evoked by the grief of this "natural death."

*For Children*
Dragonwagon, Crescent. *Winter Holding Spring.* New York: Macmillan, 1990. A lovely book, describing the "winter" of grief of a widowed father and daughter who find their way to a new "spring" of adjustment. (5–8 years)
Lanton, Sandy. *Daddy's Chair.* Atlanta, Georgia: Kar-ben Company, 1991. The family sensitively helps a little boy to adjust to death, by gradually breaking down the psychological fence he has built around his father's favorite chair.

*On AIDS*
Brans, Jo, and Margaret Taylor Smith. *Mother, I Have Something to Tell You.* Garden City, NY: Doubleday, 1987. Written from a homosexual point of view, this explains that lifestyle to parents who have not confronted the issue of their offspring's sexual preference before.

*On Funerals*
Consumer Reports editors. *Funerals: Consumers' Last Rights.* New York: Random House, 1977. A complete analysis of the options available by the reputed consumer protection group.

Nelson, Thomas. *It's Your Choice*. Washington, D.C.: American Association of Retired Persons, 1982. Describes the options currently available.

*On Suicide*

Bolton, Iris, and Mitchell, Curtis. *My Son, My Son: Healing After Suicide*. Atlanta: Bolton Press, 1990. Group techniques for grieving parents.

Geller, Norman. *The Last Teenage Suicide*. Lewiston, ME: Geller Books, 1990. Teaches high-school youth to deal with their own feelings after a friend has committed suicide and how to be active in preventing others.

Lord, Janice Harris. *No Time for Goodbyes*, 1990. Available from Compassion Book Service, Burnsville, NC. Addresses methods of dealing with the new wave of violent deaths which seem to be increasing in our society.

*On Trauma*

*For Adults*

Goldman, Linda. *Breaking the Silence: A Guide to Help Children With Complicated Grief, Suicide, Homicide, AIDS, Violence, and Abuse*. Levitown, PA: Accelerated Development, 1996. A tremendously reader-friendly guide for parents, educators, and anyone working with grieving children.

Hicks, Robert. *Failure to Scream*. Nashville, TN: Nelson Publishing.

Johnson, Joy. *Keys to Teaching Children About Death and Grief*. New York, NY: Barron's Publishing, 1999. Another easy-to read book for families and caregivers, including chapters on helping children deal with trauma.

Miller, Karen. *The Crisis Manual: 76 Crisis Manual for Early Childhood Teachers: How to Handle the Really Difficult Problems*. Beltsville, MD: Gryphon House Books, 1995. Especially written for early childhood teachers, this is an excellent resource for educators, covering many difficult situations from illness, violent death to abuse.

Volpe, Joseph; Lerner, Mark; and Lindell, Brad. *A Practical Guide to Crisis Response in Our Schools*. Commack, NJ: American Academy of Experts in Traumatic Stress.

*For Children*

Salloum, Alison. *Reactions.* Omaha, NE. Centering Corporation, Box 4600, Omaha, NE 68104 Phone: 402-553-1200. 1998. A workbook to help young people who are experiencing trauma and grief. Excellent resource for any type of violence. (8-18 years)

## For Children

*General*

Berger, Terry. *I Have Feelings.* New York: Human Sciences Press, 1971. An illustrated explanation for the 4- to 8-year-old that ugly feelings are as valid as beautiful ones.

Bernstein, Joanne. *Loss and How to Cope with It.* New York: Seabury Press, 1977. A straightforward address, in language suitable for the middle schooler.

Heegaard, Marge. *When Something Terrible Happens: Children Learn to Cope with Grief.* Minneapolis, MN: Woodland Press, 1992. A workbook for grieving children. Covers a lot of difficult situations and allows good creativity from the child. (6-12 years)

Miles, Miska. *Annie and the Old One.* Boston, MA: Houghton, Mifflin, 1971. A much beloved fictional classic recounting an Indian grandmother's explanation of death to a young child. (8–12 years)

Salloum, Alison. *Reactions.* Omaha, NE: Centering Corporation (www.centering.org), 1998. A workbook to help young people (ages 8 through 18) through trauma and grief.

Stein, Sara Bonnett. *About Dying: An Open Family Book for Parent and Child.* New York: Walker & Co., 1974. A beautifully illustrated book for parent and child, explaining the role of death in the life cycle.

White, E. B. *Charlotte's Web.* New York: Harper & Row, 1952. A fictional account of a little spider's courage. (5 years up)

Williams, Margery. *The Velveteen Rabbit.* Boston, MA: David Godine, 1956. A fairy tale about a manufactured pet rabbit, who becomes so old he is lost to his youthful master. (kindergarten)

*About Aging*

Blue, Rose. *Grandma Didn't Wave Back.* New York: Dell, 1972. Explaining the changes in a beloved grandmother's personality. (7–10 years)

De Paola, Tomie. *Nana Upstairs, Nana Downstairs.* New York: Putnam, 1973. When grandma "upstairs" finally dies, grandma "downstairs" is now old enough to take her place. (kindergarten–7 years)

Fassler, Joan. *My Grandpa Died Today.* New York: Human Sciences Press, 1971. Recalling the sweetness of the child's relationship with grandpa before his death. (6–10 years)

### About AIDS

Because of the heavy media attention, American children are extremely aware of this topic. Some good books have already been published to provide children with non-sensational AIDS information appropriate to their age group, and more will no doubt be forthcoming. Among them are:

### For Children

Sanford, Doris. *David Has AIDS.* Portland, OR: Multinomah Press, 1989. An illustrated book for 5- to 8-year-olds, which truthfully shows the decline and nondenominational faith of a normal boy, who has gotten the disease.

### For Teenagers

de St. Phalle, Niki. *AIDS: You Can't Catch It Holding Hands.* San Francisco: Lapis Press, 1987. A book that will appeal to teenagers. It tackles the subject in truthful graphic language and nonjudgmental prose, showing the tragic consequences of indiscriminate adventures.

Hyde, Margaret, and Elizabeth Forsythe. *AIDS: What Does It Mean to You?* New York: Walker & Co., 1986.

### On the Funeral

Johnson, Joy and Marv. *Tell Me Papa. Tell Me About Death and Funerals.* Omaha, NE: Centering Corp., 1978. A graphic book, with soft, wash illustrations, which show what it looks like at the funeral and at the graveside. (6–10 years)

Viorst, Judith. *The Tenth Good Thing About Barney.* New York: Atheneum, 1971. A more euphemistic story about burying a beloved cat under a tree in the garden. (6–9 years)

### Loss of a Parent

Hammond, Janice. *When My Daddy Died and When Mommy Died.* Cincinnati, OH: Cranbrook Press, 1981. Simple drawings and text for the very young child. (4 years and up)

Krementz. Jill. *How It Feels When a Parent Dies.* New York: Random House, 1981. A series of photoessays by a noted photographer, with descriptions in the children's own words. (9–12 years)

Le Shan, Eda. *Learning to Say Goodbye: When a Parent Dies.* New York: Macmillan, 1976. A gentle explanation by a psychologist. (8–10 years)

### Loss of a Sibling

Johnson, Joy and Marv. *Where's Jess?* Omaha, NE: Centering Corp., 1982. A charmingly rendered set of answers to a little girl's questions about what has happened to her baby sister. (3–5 years)

Lee, Virginia. *The Magic Moth.* New York: Seabury Press, 1972. A fictional classic of terminal illness and death, seen through the eyes of a young brother. (8–11 years)

Levy, Erin Linn. *Children Are Not Paper Dolls.* Barrington, Illinois: The Publishers Mark, 1982. A coloring book for children ages 6 and up that can help them express their feelings of grief and anger when a brother or sister dies.

Sims, Alicia. *Am I Still a Sister?* Albuquerque, NM: Big A and Company, 1988. A young girl with whom youngsters can identify, vividly describes how she feels when her sibling dies.

### Loss of a Friend

Cohen, Janice. *I Had a Friend Named Peter.* New York: Morrow, 1987. A beautifully illustrated book by an experienced counselor which will help children deal with this sensitive topic.

### For Adolescents

Craven, Margaret. *I Heard the Owl Call My Name.* New York: Dell, 1973. A young priest learns from the Alaskan Indians he serves how to regard his own life and death. (fiction)

Gunther, John. *Death Be Not Proud.* New York: Harper & Row, 1971. A beautifully-written account of a teenager's decline from a brain tumor. This book is still much beloved. (nonfiction)

Lund, Doris. *Eric.* New York: Dell, 1974. How Eric lived to the fullest before he died, described by his mother. (nonfiction)

*Re-Marriage*
Green, Phyllis. *A New Mother for Martha.* New York: Human Sciences Press, 1978. Martha creates a shrine to her dead mother at home and resents the presence of a new woman in the house. (Fiction)

*Support Groups*
*The Candlelighters.* Childhood Cancer Foundation, 7910 Woodmont Avenue, Suite 460, Bethesda, MD 20814. For parents of children with cancer.
*Children's Hospital International.* 901 North Washington Street, Alexandria, VA 22314. Hotline: 1-800-2-4-CHILD.
*The Compassionate Friends.* P.O. Box 1347. Oak Brook, IL 60521. For parents whose children have died.
*Institute for Life-Threatening Illness and Loss,* 630 West 168th Street, New York, NY 10032.
*Mothers Against Drunk Drivers (MADD).* 5330 Primrose, Suite 146, Fair Oaks, CA 95628.
*Mothers of AIDS Patients,* c/o Barbara Peabody, 3403 E. Street, San Diego, CA 92102.
*National AIDS Information Clearing House* has a toll-free AIDS hotline: 1-800-458-5231. Call for basic information materials.
*National Catholic Ministry to the Bereaved.* 7835 Harvard Avenue, Cleveland, OH 44105.
*National Sudden Infant Death Foundation.* 310 S. Michigan Ave., Chicago, IL 60604. Conducts research, offers preventive assistance, and aids the bereaved.
*Parents of Murdered Children.* 1739 Bella Vista, Cincinnati, OH 45237.
*Pediatric AIDS Foundation,* 2407 Wilshire Boulevard, Suite 613, Santa Monica, CA 90403. Hotline: 1-800-488-5000.

# Index

**A**

accidental death, 58-59, 179
adults to children, 85-87. *See also*
    language of/for child
afterlife questions, 40-41
age of child, 11
    crisis characteristics to
        remember, 175-79
    nine to twelve years, 21-23,
        117-18, 178-79
    six to nine years, 20-21, 115-17,
        177-78
    teenagers. *See* teenagers
    two to six years, 16-20, 112-15,
        175-77
AIDS, 70-72
    anger of survivors, 71, 74, 76
    fear of, 71, 76, 79
    how to tell children, 75-77
    knowledge of children, 73-74
    parents with AIDS, 72-73
    privacy and community, 78-79
    reactions of children, 77-78
    stigma of, 78-79
angels and clouds, 17-18, 26
anger, 24, 42, 66-67, 71, 74, 76,
    79-80
    grieving process and, 119-23

    reasons for anger (checklist),
        184-85
    animal, death of, 93-94
    art therapy, 88-89

**B**

bed-wetting, 156
Bergson, Lisa, 67-68
blaming self, 1, 5, 13, 18-19, 113
Bowlby, John, 107
Brody, Jane, 69
Brogan, John, 63
*Buffalo News*, 57
Butherus, Constance, 91-92

**C**

Callahan, Dolores, 41
child, death of, 41-42, 44, 46
    family member. *See* family member,
        death of
    friend or classmate, 55-57
    infant death, 47-55. *See also*
        infant death
classmate's death, 55-57
Cohen, Carol, 72, 75
Coleman, Gary, 158
Columbine High School shootings,
    133
communication contract, 28, 33-34

Compassionate Friends, 45, 56
contagiousness, 20-21
crisis checklists
  age nine to twelve, 178-79
  age six to nine, 177-78
  age three to six, 176-77
  death, meaning of, 174-75
  describing how/why of death to
    children, 179-80
  funeral descriptions, 181-83
  initial reactions to telling
    child, 172-73
  newborn to age three, 175-76
  reactions of children, 183-86
  sadness, understanding of, 173
  teenagers, 179

**D**
Dane, Barbara, 76, 77-78
Danto, Bruce, 6, 16, 66-67
"dead," 7, 28-29, 30-32, 174-75
death, views of. See also specific
  contexts, ages, and subject
  headings
  afterlife questions, 40-41
  anger. See anger
  connecting events, 18-20
  contagious death, 20-21
  crisis checklists, 174-75
  details, interest in, 11-12,
    22-23
  euphemisms, avoidance of, 30-32,
    81
  explicit information, 11-12
  fantasies, 4-6, 13-14, 18-20
  grieving. See grieving
  guilt and responsibility. See
    guilt
  language to use with children,
    174-75. See also language
    of/for child
  magical thinking, 18, 23, 113-14
  meaning of death, 7, 28-29,
    30-32, 174-75
  personified death, 20
  practical concerns, 22-23
  punishment, death as, 21-22

  religious concepts, 31-32
  reversible view, 17-18
  scientific knowledge, 22
  six- to nine-year-old children,
    20-21, 177-78
  sleeping, 31-32
  teenagers, 24
  theories in middle years, 22
  transience of life, 24
  two- to six-year-old children,
    16-20, 175-77
Death of a Child, The (Typond), 42
De Bernardo, Francis, 55-56
denial, 86-87
destructive behavior, 101-2
Devlin, Jim, 55
"Different Strokes" (TV show), 158
disease. See illness and disease
Dougy Center (Portland, OR), 80-81

**E**
Elliott, Barbara, 49
emotions, showing of
  anger. See anger
  explaining, 33
  grandparent's death, 32-33
  grieving process and. See
    grieving
employment. See workplace
euphemisms, avoidance of, 30-32, 81
Evans, Beth, 90, 93
exhaustion, 98
Explaining Death to Children
  (Grollman), 160
explanations. See language of child

**F**
family blueprints, 26-27
family member, death of
  AIDS. See AIDS
  anticipatory grief, 47
  grandparent's death. See
    grandparent's death
  grieving, ritual of, 46. See also
    grieving
  murder. See murder
  parent's death. See parent's

death
  sibling's death, 41-42, 44, 46
  stablity, maintaining, 44-46
  suicide. *See* suicide
  traumatic stress. *See* traumatic
    stress
fantasies, 4-6, 13-14
  connecting events, 18-20
  contagious death, 20-21
  grieving process, in, 113-15
  personification, 20
  word confusion, 21
fear
  AIDS, of, 71, 76, 79
  art therapy for, 88-89
  sleep, of, 21
  traumatic stress symptoms, 156
Fishkin, Hal, 13, 14, 23, 59-60,
  61-62, 65, 111, 164-65
forever, concepts of, 36-37
friend's death, 55-57
funerals, 34-35, 46-47, 158-61
  body, viewing of, 161-65
  choice of attendance for child,
    159-61
  good-bye gift, 162, 165-66
  infant death, 51, 55
  murder victim, 61
  preparing children for, 161-65,
    181-83
  questions and answers, 167-68
Furman, Edna, 49-50

**G**
Gordon, Audrey, 58, 109, 124
grandparent's death
  afterlife questions, 40-41
  disease or illness, 29
  emotions, showing of, 32-33
  euphemisms, avoidance of, 30-32
  events, explanations of, 34-35
  frankness, degrees of, 30
  funerals, 34-35
  old age, 28
  questions to expect, 36-40
  telling the child, 27-30
gray hair, 19

grieving, 95-98
  advice from others, 126-28
  anger and, 119-23
  anticipatory grief, 47
  avoidance, 105
  children's special needs, 103-6
  continuity of care for children,
    125-26
  dependency, 99
  destructive behavior, 101-2
  exhaustion, 98
  guilt and, 122-24. *See also* guilt
  healing. *See* healing
  helping child to heal, 124-30
  hope, 110-11
  hyperactivity, 101
  letting child know what to
    expect, 128-29
  mental symptoms of, 134-35
  myths of mourning and grief, 133
  nine- to twelve-year-old children,
    117-18
  openness with children, 126-30
  pain, 110, 111-12
  panic, 99-100
  participation by child, 129-30
  physical symptoms of, 135
  preoccupation with dead person,
    100-101
  process of grieving, 106-12
  projected feelings, 104-5
  protest stage, 108-10
  regression, 102-3
  ritual and sharing in, 46
  six- to nine-year-old children,
    115-17
  support system for, 131-32,
    135-36
  teenagers, 118-19
  three stages of grief, 107-12
  traumatic stress. *See* traumatic
    stress
  two- to-six-year-old children,
    112-15
  unreality, feelings of, 99
  workplace, impact in, 136-39
Grollman, Earl, 160

guilt, 1, 5, 13, 18-19, 21-22, 24
  grieving process and, 122-24
  infant death and, 48, 52, 53, 54
  murder of parent, 61-62
  questions of self-blame, 38-39,
    113, 186
  reasons for guilt (checklist),
    185-86
  responsibility and, 186
  sibling's death, 42
  SIDS and, 52, 53, 54
  suicide, 65-66

**H**

healing
  continuity of care for children,
    125-26
  disagreement of others, 126-28
  openness with children, 126-30
  support system for, 131-32,
    135-36
HIV/AIDS. *See* AIDS
honesty and frankness, 30, 80-81
*How It Feels to Be a Child* (Klein),
  14
*How It Feels When a Parent Dies*
  (Krementz), 43
Hudson, Lisa, 144-55
hugging, 54
hyperactivity, 101

**I**

illness and disease, 29
infant death, 47-48, 179-80
  conventional coping, 47-48
  funeral for baby, 51, 55
  helping other children, 49-51,
    52-55
  questions asked by children,
    49-50
  Seeing and holding baby, 47-48,
    51
  Sudden Infant Death Syndrome
    (SIDS), 51-55, 180
  suggestions from hospital, 50-51

**J**

job. *See* workplace
*Journal of Nurse-Midwifery*, 48

**K**

Kauffman, Jeffrey, 92
Klass, Dennis, 58, 109, 124
Klein, Carole, 14
Krementz, Jill, 43
Kushner, Harold, 58

**L**

language of/for child, 14. *See also*
    specific concepts, events and
    questions
  afterlife questions, 40-41
  angels and clouds, 17-18, 26
  euphemisms, avoidance of, 30-32,
    81
  explaining "dead" to child,
    174-75
  fantasies of death. *See* fantasies
  funeral situations, explanations
    of, 181-83
  how and why of death, checklist
    for explaining, 179-80
  miscarriage, 179-80
  murder, 180
  not knowing what to say, 84-85
  SIDS, 180
  stillborn, 180
  suicide, 180
  terminal illness, 179
  word confusion and fantasy, 21
Lee, Will, 7
Leeuwenburgh, Erica, 83
Lefebvre, Leo, 124
Lindeman, Erich, 61, 111
Lipson, Michael, 72, 73, 75
loneliness of kids, 2-3, 6
Longpré, Elise, 45
lying to child, 80-81

**M**

magical thinking, 18, 23, 113-14
Maiden, Ula, 63

managers and supervisors. *See* workplace
Manning, Doug, 108, 160
Mayer-Avedon Women's Support Group (New York), 80
mentally retarded child, 91-92
Meyers, Barbara, 93-94
*Minister Speaks About Funerals, A* (Manning), 108, 160
miscarriage, 179-80
misunderstandings, 15-16
*Monitor*, 60
morality, sense of, 21
Moses, Ken, 87
Mothers Against Drunk Drivers (MADD), 45, 58
Motta, Robert, 157
murder, 59-62, 180

**N**
neglecting children, 81-82
Nenner, Fred, 142-43
neutral party, 82-83
*Newsday Magazine*, 166
*New York Times, The*, 67-68, 69
not knowing what to say, 84-85

**O**
Oberman, Mark, 166
Oklahoma City bombing, 133
old age, 28, 36-37, 179
one day at a time, 85-86
other people
  disagreement from, 126-28
  resistance to telling children, 172
  support systems. *See* support system

**P**
panic, 99-100
parent's death, 42-45
  murder of parent, 59-62
  suicide. *See* suicide
  traumatic stress from. *See* traumatic stress
Patterson, Paul, 43-44, 47

*Pediatrics* magazine, 49
Pentagon attack, 133
*Peoplemaking* (Satir), 24-25
Peretz, David, 68
personifications of death, 20
pet, death of, 93-94
Post-Traumatic Stress Disorder (PTSD), 139-42
Pouissant, Alvin, 60
preoccupation with dead person, 100-101
protection from truth, 79-81
protector, child as, 88
Pynoos, Robert, 60

**Q**
Quirk, Tina Russo, 48

**R**
Rando, Therese, 133, 141
regression, 102-3, 148, 156
regrets, 83-84
religious concepts, 31-32, 144
  afterlife questions, 40-41
responsibility for death, 186. *See* also guilt
Rosenberg, Pat Travis, 169-70
Rothbart-Mayer, Ruth, 74, 75, 76, 78-79, 80, 84-85

**S**
sadness, understanding of, 173
St. John's Hospital (Springfield, IL), 50-51
Satir, Virginia, 24-25
Schneidman, Edwin, 63
schools
  death in, 55-57
  informing school of death, 90-91
  support system in grieving, 90, 136, 155
  trauma response and support from, 155-57
Schuurman, Donna, 80-81
Schwartz-Borden, Gwen, 111, 112, 113, 121, 126
secrets, 13-14, 74, 87-88

self-blame. *See* guilt
"Sesame Street" (TV show), 7, 29
sheltering kids, 1-7
sibling, death of, 41-42, 44, 46
  infant death. *See* infant death
Singer, Dulcy, 7
sleep
  death as sleep, 31-32
  fear of, 21
  problems with, 19, 52, 53
Smith-Torres, Carol, 160
Snyder, Barbara, 57
Solomon, Judy, 89
stoplight model, 85-87
Stouffer, Jack, 86
sudden death, 55-57
  accidental death, 58-59, 179
  Sudden Infant Death Syndrome
    (SIDS), 51-55, 180
suicide, 62-65, 140, 180
  children, suicides of, 69-70
  emotional problems and reactions
    to, 65-69
  "follow the leader" syndrome,
    68-69
  note, reading of, 66-67
  stigma associated with, 63, 67-68
support system, 90, 131-32, 135-36
  schools, crisis response from,
    90, 136, 155-57
  support groups, listing of, 196
  traumatic stress approaches,
    142-44

T
*Tablet, The* newspaper, 55
talking. *See* death, views of;
    language of/for child; specific
    subject headings
teachers. *See also* schools
  death of, 55-56
  support system in grieving, 90,
    136
teenagers, 104, 179
  grief, processing of, 118-19
  guidance for, 24
  suicides among, 69-70

television, 7, 12
terminal illness, 179
*Thanatos* journal, 41, 45
therapy, 82-83, 123, 148, 154, 186
  art therapy, 88-89
  murder of parent, after, 62
  suicide, coping with, 64, 68-69
*They Need to Know* (Gordon and
    Klass), 58, 109, 124
thumb-sucking, 156
Toffler, Alvin, 159
traumatic stress, 139
  child's experience, 149-52
  comfort zone for caregiver,
    142-43
  personal narrative of, 144-55
  Post-Traumatic Stress Disorder
    (PTSD), 139-42
  schools, support from, 155-57
  support system approaches, 142-44
  what to avoid, 144, 153-54
  what to do and say, 143-44,
    148-53
*Treatment for Complicated Mourning*
    (Rando), 133
Troescher, Carol, 57
Turkington, Carol, 60
Typond, Claudia, 42

W
waiting too long, 83-84
wakes. *See* funerals
wanting to know, 80-81
what to say, not knowing, 84-85.
    *See also* language of/for child
*When Bad Things Happen to Good
    People* (Kushner), 58
whispers and secrets, 13-14, 74,
    87-88
World Trade Towers attack, 133

Z
Zamierowski, Margaret, 89
Zicherman, Barrie Sue, 136

# About the Authors

DAN SCHAEFER, PH.D., is an internationally recognized author, speaker, and management consultant, assisting individuals and corporations with strategies for performance enhancement, stress management, and the reduction of the impact of loss and life transition in the workplace. *How Do We Tell the Children,* now in its third edition, is drawn from Dan's experience in assisting individuals in acute grief.

Dr. Schaefer has served as a guest faculty member at the College of Physicians and Surgeons, Columbia University, and the graduate schools at New York University, Adelphi, Rutgers, and Hofstra University. He is a consultant to national, state, and local agencies, including the New York City Health and Hospitals Corporation, New York City Board of Eduction, New Jersey League of Municipalities, Veterans Administration Health Care System, Survivors of the Shield, and TAPS, an organization serving survivors of military loss. Dan is also a member of the American Society of Training and Development and the Institute of Management Consultants.

To contact the author, please call (212) 265-1888, e-mail danconco@msn.com, or write to: Dan Schaefer, Ph.D., Peak Performance Strategies, 161 West 61st Street, New York, NY 10023.

CHRISTINE LYONS is a journalist and reporter whose work has appeared in *The New York Times* and *The New York Post,* among other publications. She lives in New York City.

# Parenting and Childcare Books

## BABY MASSAGE
Parent–Child Bonding Through Touch
**Amelia D. Auckett**
**Introduction by Dr. Tiffany Field**
128 pp. 5½" x 8¼". 34 b&w photos and drawings. Bibliography, Index.
**1-55704-022-2. $11.95. PB.**

## BEYOND THE BIG TALK
A Parent's Guide to Raising Sexually Healthy Children—from Middle School to High School and Beyond
**Debra W. Haffner, M.P.H.**
256 pp. 6" x 9".
**1-55704-517-8. $15.95. PB.**
**1-55704-472-4. $24.95. HC.**

## FROM DIAPERS TO DATING
A Parent's Guide to Raising Sexually Healthy Children—from Infancy to Middle School
**Debra W. Haffner, M.P.H.**
240 pp. 6" x 9".
**1-55704-426-0. $14.95. PB.**
**1-55704-385-X. $23.95. HC.**

## HOW DO WE TELL THE CHILDREN?
A Step-by-Step Guide for Helping Children Two to Teen Cope When Someone Dies
**Daniel Schaefer, Ph.D., and Christine Lyons**
224 pp. 5½" x 8¼".
Quick-reference Crisis Checklist, Index.
**1-55704-425-2. $14.95. PB.**
**1-55704-430-9. $24.95. HC.**

## HOW TO HELP YOUR CHILD OVERCOME YOUR DIVORCE
A Support Guide For Families
**Elissa P. Benedek, M.D.,**
**and Catherine F. Brown**
336 pp. 6" x 9".
**1-55704-461-9. $15.95. PB.**

## INNER BEAUTY, INNER LIGHT
Yoga for Pregnant Women
**Frederick Leboyer, M.D.**
**Introduction by B. K. S. Iyengar**
256 pp. 8" x 10⅞". 100 b&w photos.
**1-55704-315-9. $18.95. PB.**

## KEEP YOUR KIDS TOBACCO-FREE
Smart Strategies for Parents of Children Ages 3 Through 19
**Robert Schwebel, Ph.D.**
192 pp. 5⅜" x 8". Bibliography, Index.
**1-55704-369-8. $14.95. PB.**
**1-55704-368-X. $19.95. HC.**

## KIDS & SPORTS
Everything You and Your Child Need to Know About Sports, Physical Activity, and Good Health—A Doctor's Guide for Parents and Coaches
**Eric Small, M.D., FAAP**
192 pp. 6" x 9". 10 b&w illustrations.
**1-55704-498-8. $24.95. HC.**

## LOVING HANDS
The Traditional Art of Baby Massage
**Frederick Leboyer, M.D.**
144 pp. 8" x 10⅞". 70 b&w photos.
**1-55704-314-0. $16.95. PB.**

## MOMMY, MY HEAD HURTS
A Doctor's Guide To Your Child's Headache
**Sarah Cheyette, M.D.**
208 pp. 5¼" x 8". Diagrams, Index.
**1-55704-471-6. $22.95. HC.**

## MOTHERING THE NEW MOTHER
Women's Feelings and Needs After Childbirth: A Support, Resource Guide
**Sally Placksin**
420 pp. 6" x 9". Resources, Bibliography, Index.
**1-55704-317-5. $18.95. PB.**

## RAISING YOUR JEWISH/CHRISTIAN CHILD
How Interfaith Parents Can Give Children the Best of Both Their Heritages
**Lee F. Gruzen**
288 pp. 5⅜" x 8". Bibliography, Checklists, Index.
**1-55704-414-7. $16.95. PB.**

## THE READY-TO-READ, READY-TO-COUNT HANDBOOK
How to Best Prepare Your Child for School—A Parent's Guide
**Teresa Savage**
288 pp. 5¼" x 8". Bibliography, Games, Illustrations, Index, Resources.
**1-55704-413-9. $16.95. PB.**

## SAYING NO IS NOT ENOUGH, 2ND ED.
Helping Your Kids Make Wise Decisions About Alcohol, Tobacco, and Other Drugs
**Robert Schwebel, Ph.D.**
**Introduction by Benjamin Spock, M.D.**
192 pp. 5½" x 8". Bibliography, Index.
**1-55704-318-3. $14.95. PB.**

# from Newmarket Press

## LYNDA MADARAS

### MY BODY, MY SELF FOR BOYS
A "What's Happening to My Body?" Activity Book
for Pre-Teens and Teens
**Lynda Madaras & Area Madaras**
112 pp. 7¼" x 9". Over 60 drawings & photos.
**1-55704-440-6. $12.95. PB.**

### MY BODY, MY SELF FOR GIRLS
A "What's Happening to My Body?" Activity Book
for Pre-Teens and Teens
**Lynda Madaras & Area Madaras**
128 pp. 7¼" x 9". Over 40 drawings.
**1-55704-441-4. $12.95. PB.**

### MY FEELINGS, MY SELF
**Journal for Girls**
**Lynda Madaras & Area Madaras**
160 pp. 7¼" x 9". 30 drawings. Bibliography.
**1-55704-442-2. $12.95 PB.**

### THE "WHAT'S HAPPENING TO MY BODY?" BOOK FOR BOYS, 3RD ED.
**Lynda Madaras with Area Madaras**
**Foreword by Martin Anderson, M.D.**
288 pp. 5¼" x 8". 48 drawings. Bibliography, Index.
**1-55704-443-0. $12.95. PB.**
**1-55704-447-3. $22.95. HC.**

### THE "WHAT'S HAPPENING TO MY BODY?" BOOK FOR GIRLS 3RD ED.
**Lynda Madaras with Area Madaras**
304 pp. 5¼" x 8". 51 drawings. Bibliography, Index.
**1-55704-444-9. $12.95. PB.**
**1-55704-448-1. $22.95. HC.**

## YOUR CHILD AT PLAY SERIES

### IN TIME AND WITH LOVE
Caring for Infants and Toddlers With Special
Needs
**Marilyn Segal, Ph.D., with Roni Leiderman,
Ph.D., and Wendy Masi, Ph.D.**
208 pp. 7¼" x 9". Bibliography, Resources, Index.
**1-55704-445-7. $18.95. PB.**

### YOUR CHILD AT PLAY: BIRTH TO ONE YEAR
Discovering the Senses and Learning About the
World
**Marilyn Segal, Ph.D.**
352 pp. 7¼" x 9". 183 photos. Bibliography, Index.
**1-55704-330-2. $17.95. PB.**
**1-55704-334-5. $27.95. HC.**

### YOUR CHILD AT PLAY: ONE TO TWO YEARS
Exploring, Learning, Making Friends, and
Pretending
**Marilyn Segal, Ph.D.**
304 pp. 7¼" x 9". 242 photos. Bibliography, Index.
**1-55704-331-0. $16.95. PB.**
**1-55704-335-3. $27.95. HC.**

### YOUR CHILD AT PLAY: TWO TO THREE YEARS
Growing Up, Language, and the Imagination
**Marilyn Segal, Ph.D.**
240 pp. 7¼" x 9". 132 photos. Bibliography, Index.
**1-55704-332-9. $16.95. PB.**
**1-55704-336-1. $27.95. HC.**

### YOUR CHILD AT PLAY: THREE TO FIVE YEARS
Conversation, Creativity, and Learning Letters,
Words, and Numbers
**Marilyn Segal, Ph.D.**
**Foreword by Wendy Masi, Ph.D.**
304 pp. 7¼" x 9". 120 photos. Bibliography, Index.
**1-55704-333-7. $16.95. PB.**
**1-55704-337-X. $27.95. HC.**

### YOUR CHILD AT PLAY: FIVE TO EIGHT YEARS
Building Friendships, Expanding Interests, and
Resolving Conflicts
**Marilyn Segal, Ph.D., and Betty Bardige, Ed.D.**
**Foreword by Samuel Meisels, Ph.D.**
256 pp. 7¼" x 9". 89 photos and drawings.
**1-55704-401-5. $17.95. PB.**
**1-55704-402-3. $29.95. HC.**

# PARENTING/CHILDCARE BOOKS FROM NEWMARKET PRESS

Ask for these titles at your local bookstore or use this coupon and enclose a check or money order payable to: **Newmarket Press**, 18 East 48th Street, New York, NY 10017.

**Amelia D. Auckett**
*Baby Massage*
____ $11.95 pb (1-55704-022-2)

**Elissa P. Benedek, M.D., and Catherine F. Brown, M.Ed.**
*How to Help Your Child Overcome Your Divorce*
____ $15.95 pb (1-55704-461-9)

**Sarah Cheyette, M.D.**
*Mommy, My Head Hurts: A Doctor's Guide to Your Child's Headaches*
____ $21.95 hc (1-55704-471-6)

**Lee F. Gruzen**
*Raising Your Jewish/Christian Child*
____ $16.95 pb (1-55704-414-7)

**Debra W. Haffner, M.P.H.**
*Beyond The Big Talk: Every Parent's Guide to Raising Sexually Healthy Teens*
____ $24.95 hc (1-55704-472-4)
____ $15.95 pb (1-55704-517-8)
*From Diapers to Dating: A Parent's Guide to Raising Sexually Healthy Children*
____ $23.95 hc (1-55704-385-X)
____ $14.95 pb (1-55704-426-0)

**Frederick Leboyer, M.D.**
*Inner Beauty, Inner Light: Yoga for Pregnant Women*
____ $18.95 pb (1-55704-315-9)
*Loving Hands: Traditional Baby Massage*
____ $16.95 pb (1-55704-314-0)

**Lynda Madaras & Area Madaras**
*My Body, My Self for Boys*
____ $12.95 pb (1-55704-440-6)
*My Body, My Self for Girls*
____ $12.95 pb (1-55704-441-4)
*My Feelings, My Self*
____ $12.95 pb (1-55704-442-2)
*The What's Happening to My Body? Book for Boys*
____$22.95 hc (1-55704-447-3)
____$12.95 pb (1-55704-443-0)
*The What's Happening to My Body? Book for Girls*
____ $22.95 hc (1-55704-448-1)
____ $12.95 pb (1-55704-444-9)

**Sally Placksin**
*Mothering the New Mother, Rev. Ed.*
____ $18.95 pb (1-55704-317-5)

**Teresa Savage**
*The Ready-to-Read, Ready-to-Count Handbook*
____ $16.95 pb (1-55704-413-9)

**Dan Schaefer & Christine Lyons**
*How Do We Tell the Children?, 3rd Ed.*
____ $24.95 hc (1-55704-430-9)
____ $14.95 pb (1-55704-425-2)

**Robert Schwebel, Ph.D.**
*Keep Your Kids Tobacco-Free*
____ $14.95 pb (1-55704-369-8)
*Saying No Is Not Enough, Rev. Ed.*
____ $14.95 pb (1-55704-318-3)

**Marilyn Segal, Ph.D.**
*In Time and With Love*
____ $18.95 pb (1-55704-445-7)
*Your Child at Play: Birth to One Year, 2nd Ed.*
. ____ $27.95 hc (1-55704-334-5)
____ $17.95 pb (1-55704-330-2)
*Your Child at Play: One to Two Years, 2nd Ed.*
____ $27.95 hc (1-55704-335-3)
____ $16.95 pb (1-55704-331-0)
*Your Child at Play: Two to Three Years, 2nd Ed.*
____ $27.95 hc (1-55704-336-1)
____ $16.95 pb (1-55704-332-9)
*Your Child at Play: Three to Five Years, 2nd Ed.*
____ $27.95 hc (1-55704-337-X)
____ $16.95 pb (1-55704-333-7)
*Your Child at Play: Five to Eight Years, 2nd Ed.*
____ $29.95 hc (1-55704-402-3)
____ $17.95 pb (1-55704-401-5)

**Eric Small**
*Kids & Sports*
____ $24.95 pb (1-55704-498-8)

---

For postage and handling, please add $3.50 for the first book, plus $1.00 for each additional book. Prices and availability are subject to change.

I enclose a check or money order payable to **Newmarket Press** in the amount of $ _____

Name _____

Address _____

City/State/Zip _____

**For discounts on orders of five or more copies or to get a catalog**, contact Newmarket Press, Special Sales Department, 18 East 48th Street, New York, NY 10017; phone: 212-832-3575 or 1-800-669-3903; fax: 212-832-3629; or e-mail: sales@newmarketpress.com.